What Your Realtor, Loan Officer and Appraiser Forgot to Tell You!

A Guide for First Time Home Buyers

by

Richard S. Kosoff

authorHOUSE™

1663 Liberty Drive, Suite 200
Bloomington, Indiana 47403
(800) 839-8640
www.AuthorHouse.com

First published by AuthorHouse 12/03/05

ISBN: 1-4208-3742-7 (sc)

Printed in the United States of America
Bloomington, Indiana

This book is printed on acid-free paper.

Edited By: Ronald H Epstein
Cover Design By: Linda H Kosoff

Contact the author at: _rkmortgage@earthlink.net_

To Nikki and Mikey,
my greatest source of inspiration.

TABLE OF CONTENTS

WHO AM I?

In California, when we say "yard," we mean it literally.

I started in the Real Estate business in 1987. Back then I was hired by Home Fed. Bank and was trained as an appraiser. In 1990, I switched companies and appraised for Citibank. In mid-1991, I attended a Citibank meeting with the mortgage loan officers at an offsite hotel. They had breakfast, omelets, fresh fruit, rolls and warm muffins. They laughed and appeared to be having much fun, a lot more fun than any meeting I had attended with the appraisers. That was it. In 1991, after already passing several appraisal competency exams, I decided to jump to the loan origination department and start over as a home loan officer for Citibank. I worked there until 1993, when I was offered a position with PNCMortgage, one of the biggest regional banks in the country. In 1997, I was made an Area Sales Manager and still maintained my production. In 1998 and 1999, I was the top loan officer for PNC in Southern California. In February 2001, the mortgage division of PNC was purchased by Washington Mutual, where I maintained my production and continued making President's Club, an honor awarded to less than 5% of the company nationwide. In that time, I can truly say that I've learned a few things that I'm happy to share.

By the time you get done reading this book you will understand the home buying process from selecting an agent, selecting and qualifying for the right loan, avoiding being an easy mark for the unscrupulous and saving a lot of money.

Real estate is the best game in town! Of course, people need a place to sleep, but real estate offers so much more: tax write-offs, a hedge against inflation, a savings plan and potential large returns on your investment are a few facts that come to mind. Best of all is that you get all of these things today with as little as 20%, 5%, 3% and even 0% down. How many investments can promise that? There's lots to talk about, but for now welcome to the best game on earth: real estate.

REAL ESTATE – THE PLAN

"Would you like to purchase a 'No Solicitor' sign?"

YOU'VE GOT TO HAVE A PLAN. Where does it start? I suppose it might start one Sunday morning when you are sitting around looking at the newspaper. Suddenly the Real Estate section falls out onto your lap and a picture of a new, beautiful Spanish-style home is staring at you. You're working! You're making money! And if you have to listen to those bratty kids in the next apartment one more time, you'll scream. Not to mention how much you are paying for this dump. Then it hits you! "Let's call an agent. Let's buy something. We can afford it if we can pay for this. Plus I hear it's a good tax write-off, a good stepping stone, and a good investment plan." HOLD ON THERE!

Before you reach for that phone on the second biggest decision of your life, you are going to need a plan. And this plan is good if you are a first-time buyer or have decided to move up. Of course, if you already own a home, you may already feel comfortable with the process. Use this book as a refresher course. Maybe it can help you point out your successes and failures the first time out.

Here it is, The Plan:

1) Make a budget to see where your income is spent.
2) Determine how much money you have for your new mortgage payment.
3) Use this book to determine how much of a mortgage you can handle.

4) Determine how much money you have saved for the down payment.
5) Add the down payment to the loan amount to determine your sales price.
6) Call a Lender. Have your credit checked and get PRE-APPROVED.
7) Make a list of areas in which you'd like to live.
8) Use the newspaper to determine if these areas have homes in your price range.
9) Find an agent, find a home inspector, and find an escrow company.
10) Buy a home, get fire insurance.
11) Be nervous – it's OK. It's a big decision.
12) Be happy – you're living the American Dream.

Therefore, I've written this book in this order. First the loan, then the agent. Trust me, it's a lot less stressful looking at houses when you know you can afford to buy them. In fact, most sellers will not even consider an offer unless it comes with a bonafide pre-approval letter. A pre-approval letter comes from a reputable lender and confirms that your credit has been reviewed, you spoke to a professional and that you can afford to buy the house on which you are writing an offer.

THE LOAN PROCESS

Maybe you have a good friend or family member in the mortgage profession. If so, that's great. He or she can ask you all of the appropriate financial questions, get you pre-approved and into your first home. If you don't have a friend in the business, then you're wise to do a little research. This can be a daunting process. It can be expensive and, for some, even more expensive. There are many options to getting a loan and many terms to confound you. By reading this book you have decided to be a *partner* in the home buying process and not a mere participant. The difference is between one who buys a home and one who is put in a home. If you are like me, your funds are limited and throwing money away is not something you relish. A hundred dollars in my pocket is a lot more valuable than in the lender's pocket. Of course, I'm kidding when I say hundreds. Apathy can cost you thousands.

The following pages don't explain everything, just the information you need to understand the complexity of the mortgage industry and the information you need to make a good decision.

Where Do I Start?

Find a good loan officer. That's a BIGGIE. A good loan officer will be a good listener. He will get you the loan that you want and not the one that earns him a bigger commission. He will communicate with you often and keep you well informed as to where the loan is in the system. He will discuss the costs of the loan with you, and these costs will be reasonable when compared to other lenders. This being said, let's look at where these individuals reside and how their roles differ.

Direct Lenders, Mortgage Bankers and Mortgage Brokers

Direct Lenders – A direct lender implies a loan officer who works for a bank that lends its own money. It's based on the old concept of "put your money here (i.e. into a savings account) and we will lend it out to other clients (in the form of mortgages)." As such, if they lend their own money, they can write their own guidelines for whom they wish to lend to. If you have some credit issues, for instance, lenders that sell their loans to another investor may be barred from doing your loan. They can't. Your loan won't meet the credit worthiness test of the other investor and your loan will be declined regardless of your strengths (big down payment, good job). But with a direct lender, they can look to your other strengths and give less weight to your credit, thus making the loan based on their in-house guidelines.

Another nice feature from direct lenders is that they will usually check your credit and get you pre-approved for free. They are usually large institutions that will gladly pay for a copy of your credit report. It's good customer service and gives them an opportunity to win the business and do your loan.

By the way, there are few (strictly) direct lenders today. Most large institutions have both their own source of money (passbook accounts) as well as money from investors (Fannie Mae/Freddie Mac) making them both a direct lender and a mortgage banker.

Mortgage Bankers – When the bank gets its money from other investors, but lends this money in its own name, then it's acting as a mortgage banker. It's transparent to you, the consumer. You think you are getting the money for your new home from ABC Bank. In truth, ABC bank is making the loan on behalf of another investor, such as Fannie Mae and Freddie Mac.

Fannie Mae (Federal National Mortgage Association) and Freddie Mac (Federal Home Loan Mortgage Corp.) are the biggest source of investment dollars for single-family homes. These are 3/4 public and 1/4 government-owned corporations. They were established to promote home ownership by assuring a ready supply of investment dollars into mortgage-backed securities from investors all around the country (and the world). Investment houses, insurance companies, other banks and individual investors now have a place to invest their money. They can invest in Fannie and Freddie on the New York Stock Exchange. Fannie and Freddie then lend these funds to banks all around the country **that agree to make loans that meet a very specific list of requirements**. The end result has been an explosion in home ownership as banks can lend on funds other than their own. More funds to lend mean more home loans.

A loan that meets Fannie's or Freddie's list of requirements is said to **conform** to the secondary market and is therefore known as a **conforming loan**. One such requirement is that the loan is to be under $417,000 (as of January 2006). This dollar amount is determined and typically increased each year. Loans greater than $417,000 are known as jumbo loans and will have an investor other than Fannie/Freddie, a different set of qualifying guidelines and usually a little higher interest rate.

True mortgage bankers, however, may have a down side. If they always underwrite to another investor's guidelines they may not be able to meet your specific needs. For instance, let's say you had a bankruptcy a year and a half ago. Fannie and Freddie require that a BK (bankruptcy) be at least three years old before they agree to make a loan. In this case, you cannot get a Fannie or Freddie loan (ex: 30-year fixed) no matter how much money you have in savings. Today, this usually isn't a problem as many mortgage bankers are also direct lenders. For instance, if you can't get a fixed rate loan from Fannie Mae (mortgage banker), then perhaps they can offer you one of their own loan programs. It may be fixed at a higher rate or an aggressively priced, adjustable rate program. Adjustable loans are often an in-house product, also known as a portfolio product.

Mortgage Broker – This section should be entitled the Good, the Bad and the Ugly. Mortgage brokers do not have lines of credit that their underwriters write to. The money to lend does not reside with them but rather with the lender/investor that they send your mortgage loan package to. The concept is that they work on your behalf to find a lender that meets your needs based on your financial picture.

The Good – They do have a large list of investors to send your package to. As a result, if your financial picture is complicated and *if they are knowledgeable*, this may be your best plan for getting approved. The good ones will get you the best rate available.

The Bad – They can be expensive, especially if your financial picture is not that complicated. Also, since your loan is not approved in-house, there seems to be a loss of control and a loss of good information as to where your loan resides in the approval process.

The Ugly – inexperienced mortgage brokers are often caught promising the world. Their technique can be summed up by, "Let's throw it against the wall and see what sticks." The loan program, fees and rates promised have a tendency to change prior to the close of escrow. In other words, it won't be a good experience.

If you decide on a mortgage broker, my advice is to make sure that you found him or her by referral. In fact, any of the above lenders should come to you by referral but this is especially true with mortgage brokers.

Obviously, knowing the type of lender you are speaking to will help you to understand whether or not this particular lender has built in restrictions that are not disclosed to you.

In conclusion, start with a lender that will give you a free pre-approval. This means he will check your credit at no charge and tell you the level of difficulty in obtaining a loan. The more it becomes apparent that you have special circumstances, the more you may want (need) to lean towards a mortgage broker. If your financial situation is very straightforward, then you may want to speak to a mortgage banker and/or a direct lender. Also, talk to your Realtor, friends, colleagues, doctors and family members. Perhaps they can recommend a lender based on their favorable experience. Regardless, here's a list of questions to use in determining if the mortgage professional you called is good for you:

1) How long have you been doing this?
2) Where are rates going (up/down)?
3) What are your closing costs?
4) Can you lock in an interest rate for me today?
5) Can you get me pre-approved with a free credit check?
6) Am I under any obligation?
7) When we are done our discussion, can you fax me a good faith estimate of your rate, points, and closing costs?
8) What is the advantage of going with you and your bank?
9) How long will it take to get my loan fully approved?
10) Can you approve me right away over the phone?

Was Barry Kinston Lucky?

Barry Kinston came to me and needed to close quickly. He entered escrow 15 days ago and had 15 days to close on a 30-day escrow. He had a credit score of 605, not very good (we'll talk more about that later), and needed to do a low documented loan. A low documented loan is one where the client does not show his tax returns and simply states how much he earns. To make matters worse, Mr. Kinston decided to quit the auto sales business for nine months to take a class in screenwriting, which certainly did not earn him an income. Even if it did, I would not be able to use it since he did not have a history in screenwriting. Currently, he went back to selling cars for the past 2 months. On a good note, however, he was able to save a 25% down payment from the auto sales business when he was working prior to screenwriting.

In summation, I have a recently employed applicant with poor credit and no proof of current earnings, but a good down payment. Who is going to approve this?

A mortgage banker cannot do this deal. Typically, mortgage bankers approve loans based on another investor's guidelines. And those guidelines typically require some sort of continuity of employment. As a sales person, my client was 100% commission with no history of income for the past nine months. If the borrower insisted on a Fannie Mae 30-year fixed, it wasn't going to happen.

A mortgage broker might be able to do this deal, but with an awful lot of luck. Many experienced mortgage brokers, understanding the difficulty of a broken employment record, would probably bend the truth about Mr. Kinston's past. Rather than mention he took off for nine months, they might extend his previous job's employment dates to cover the missing nine months. Dishonesty will sometimes work, unless you get a good underwriter who decides to pick up the phone and verify Mr. Kingston's job stability by verifying his employment. They're suppose to. If the information can't be verified, or worse, deemed fraudulent, then the loan is immediately turned down. Do not *pass go*, do not collect $200 and do not expect to close on time.

Here comes the beauty of a Direct Lender. They have their own guidelines and can write their own rules. Furthermore, if we can't do the loan, it's much better to turn the client down in the first couple of days then a week before closing. That would at least give Mr. Kinston more time to shop other direct lenders or time to get out of the deal within the terms specified by the purchase contract. This is crucial since I'm certain Barry has no desire to sacrifice any part of the down payment that he already gave his agent when he made the offer. Typically, that equals 3% of the offer price (a.k.a. a lot of money).

As luck would have it, the sun shined on Barry Kinston that day. I picked up the phone and called the underwriter the same day he gave me his application. Based on his significant savings, the underwriter assumed that Barry was a better than average sales person in the auto business. And with 25% down, she was willing to make the deal using one of the banks own mortgage loan products. In this case, it was a very low adjustable mortgage. She dismissed the screenwriting as a personal adventure and made an exception for the large gap in employment. Barry got his home and never had to worry about wasting the agent's time, the seller's time or any part of his 3% down payment.

Pre-approved vs. Pre-qualified vs. Approved

Pre-approved implies that you have been interviewed by a mortgage professional who has also pulled your credit and is able to issue you a certificate that basically states that if the information you provided is verifiable (i.e., show paystubs, bank statements, etc.), then this lender will make you a loan. Mortgage bankers and direct lenders are the best at this since they have the authority by the lender to commit the lender to making your loan.

Pre-qualified usually implies that you had a conversation with a mortgage professional who writes a letter stating that everything sounds good pertaining to a loan, but he hasn't checked your credit. Mortgage brokers are often guilty of this because they may not feel like pulling a credit report that costs them money. In the real estate community, if the credit isn't checked, then the "pre-qualified" letter is worthless.

The best letter, of course, is the one that says you are **"Approved."** But even this letter comes with disclaimers such as "subject to a property appraisal." Nonetheless, this letter implies that you have full income and credit approval. Your income has been verified, your assets needed to close and your credit have been reviewed and your loan package has been signed-off by an underwriter. This loan is ready to close…subject to a property appraisal and clear title.

If you are ready to get (pre)approved, here are the questions you need to be prepared to answer:

1) name, social security number, current address and addresses for past 2 years
2) employment for past 2 years
3) your current income, if a salaried employee (W2)
4) your net income if self employed (before taxes) for past 2 years plus depreciation
5) bank account/liquid assets for past 2 months (name, acct number, current value)

Don't worry if your income situation is complicated. A good loan officer can either walk you through it or ask you to send your last 2 years of tax returns. Sending the returns in is an especially good idea if you have corporate returns, partnership returns and K-1's.

If you do a good job of hiding your income, you will want to make sure the lender you are talking to offers "Stated Income" or "Low Documented" loans. We'll talk more about this later.

How fast are pre-approvals? More and more mortgage professionals are able to offer free pre-approvals right over the phone, subject only to an appraisal. The advent of technology is driving the industry in this direction, which gives the consumer the ultimate confidence when shopping for a home loan. These individuals can provide you with a commitment letter guaranteeing you a loan in as little as 20 minutes. Here's how this process works:

a) An application is taken over the phone and entered in a computer.
b) A triple-merged credit report with credit score is retrieved by the computer in about two minutes.
c) Your file is electronically transferred to a central computer system that compares and weighs credit, income, loan to value, and debt ratios. All of this happens in less than 5 minutes.
d) If approved, the lender will issue a commitment letter subject to verification of the information provided and property appraisal.

It's that fast! And you can go out that day and shop with confidence. Remember, the approval is based on the information provided. Bad information, and your approval is void.

Defining a Good Borrower

Let me tell you about an early argument I had with Sally, an underwriter. (An underwriter has the authority to approve the loan for the bank). For some reason, my first client, whom I was sure was a *good borrower*, was having difficulty getting approved. The conversation went like this:

Me: Sally, what do you want? My client is putting 25% down. That's $50,000 on a $200,000 loan. (It's always nice when you make them feel as if they can't do math).

Sally: Your client was late on two car payments in the last 6 months.

Me: So what! He's putting $50,000 down and the property is appraised $10,000 over the sales price.

Sally: Your client just started his own business. How do we know he will be successful and pay us back?

Me (Still impressed that someone has saved $50,000): He's putting down $50,000 and his parents will help him out if he gets into trouble.

Sally: Declined.

There are five pieces to any loan that are required if you are to get the best rates the industry has to offer. And 4 out of the 5 specifically help define what makes a good borrower. These are the pieces to the "Home Loan Puzzle." They are:

1) your credit profile
2) income and debt ratios
3) the down payment
4) employment
5) property appraisal

Credit Profile

The first thing many companies do is to order your credit report and review your FICO score (Fair Isaac Corporation) before they do anything else. FICO scores are generated by each credit bureau. They are a numeric representation of how well you handle your financial responsibilities. Here's a quick list of the scores and how they rate:

1) 720 and above – excellent.
2) 680 to 720 – very good
3) 620 to 680 – probably have some credit issues that will require a written explanation. If the explanations are reasonable, you're still credit worthy.
4) Less than 620 – you can still get a loan with a good explanation, but probably not a (FNMA/FHLMC) fixed rate mortgage. Also, your explanations need to be excellent. The "dog ate the bill" is not going to fly. It's one thing to be late at one point in your life due to an unforeseen circumstance vs. habitually late.
5) Less than 600 – same as #4 and more difficult to get approved. You will need

some significant offsetting factors for an underwriter to approve you for a home loan.

If your credit report shows "lates" (late payments), why were you late? The goal is to establish that you had a problem one time in your life and not laziness or that you can't afford your current life style.

The following list gives you an idea as to what the credit bureaus are looking at when determining your score.

1) When do you pay your bills related to their due dates (week 1, 2, 3 or 4)?
2) How often are you late paying your bills?
3) Late paying installment debt (car, mortgage, student loans) is worse than late paying revolving debt (credit cards).
4) How late are you (30, 60, 90 days)?
5) How many credit cards do you have with balances?
6) Are your balances more or less than 50% of your maximum limit?
7) How many inquiries appear on your credit report? Inquiries are recent requests for new credit cards and/or debt.

Interesting isn't it? Having a minimum of 4 lines of debt is mandatory for most lenders to see how you pay, but have too many with balances and your credit scores will suffer. And in the mean time, how often do you go to your mailbox only to find another offer for a gold, platinum, hologram, original artwork Visa, MasterCard, Discover Card and American Express Card?

Don't have enough credit? That's OK! There are other ways to establish that you are capable of handling a significant purchase. The following creditors do not always report to the credit bureaus but absolutely may be used to show your credit worthiness. Get a credit rating from the following:

1) your landlord
2) the phone company
3) the gas company
4) your cable company
5) water and power (DWP)
6) your cell phone company
7) a pager company
8) or get 12 months of cancelled rent checks

Lenders are most interested in looking at your last two years of payment history. Installment debts are valued more than credit cards. Hence, if you have to be late on a debt one month, don't let it be the car. Size of payment does not matter vs. making the minimum payment on time and paying early. If you need to pay off a credit card to qualify, let your mortgage professional suggest this up front. Some lenders will allow it. Others will not care if you pay off a debt to qualify. When it comes to revolving debt (credit cards), some will assume that paying it off or down doesn't matter since you can run it right back up. Cars (installment debts) are a nice exception. Most banks will let you pay the car down to a remaining 10 months and will allow you to exclude these payments from your qualifying rations. Hence, it may be more advantageous to pay down the car than the credit cards. Finally, make sure you pay your rent on time. Providing 12 months of rent checks (front and back) is a great place to start and may be required by the underwriter.

John Duey is the Exception

John Duey came to me to do a mortgage. He had an OK job working as a massage therapist. He wanted to buy a home and he wanted to buy in Bel Air. Not knowing what a massage therapist makes, I went along with the pre-approval process hoping that he was the massage therapist to the stars. A pre-approval allows me to ask all of the right questions to get someone approved but more importantly, lets me check their credit.

John's credit was terrible! He had more then 21 lates in the past 2 years, which is the time frame most lenders are most interested in. Twenty-one lates! He barely paid anything on time. I knew I was in trouble.

The plot, however, thickens. John was also the heir of a major pharmaceutical company and he happened to have $6 million in the bank. Needless to say, we did the loan. $6 million is what's known in the mortgage industry as a "significant offsetting" factor. While you may not have significant assets, the bank will look for reasons why they should make the deal. But without compensating factors, you are almost guaranteed to be charged a higher interest rate, or worse, declined.

Income and Debt Ratios

Debt ratios are used to determine if your income vs. your debts, are such that a bank feels comfortable with your ability to repay a new loan.

A typical debt ratio is 33 over 38. Let's look at the 33, known as the **front-end debt ratio (FER)**.

33 or 33% means that if you take the mortgage payment including taxes and insurance, and you divide it by your income, the resulting ratio should not exceed 33%. Another way to say this is, your total mortgage payment should not exceed 1/3 your gross monthly income. If I make $6,000 a month, then the bank will allow me to buy a home with a total payment of $2,000. (2000/6000=33%). This is a conservative rule and rules always have exceptions but it's a good place for us to start.

$$\text{FER} = \frac{\text{house payment} + \text{taxes} + \text{home insurance}}{\text{Gross Income}} = 33\%$$

The back-end debt ratio should not exceed 38%. This formula is exactly the same as above but includes car payments plus credit card payments, etc., divided by your gross income.

$$BER = \frac{\text{house payment} + \text{taxes} + \text{insurance} + \text{monthly}}{\text{Gross Income}} \underline{\text{car payment, credit card, student loan payments}}$$

$$= 38\%$$

Now let's look at how debt effects this formula.

Lucy Zigbern came to me to get pre-approved to buy a home. She's a publicist for Random House and earns $90,000 a year. The house she was looking at was selling for $425,000 and Lucy was putting 20% down. Based on an interest rate of 6.5%, the following applies:

Mortgage payment including taxes and insurance
= $2,691/month
Current Gross income = 7500/month

$$FER = \frac{2,691}{7,500} = 35.8\%$$

Lucy also had student loan payments of $125/month and credit card payments of $300/month.

$$BER = \frac{\$2,691 + \$125 + 300}{\$7,500} = \frac{\$3,116}{\$7,500} = 41.5\%$$

Now Lucy has a Back End Debt Ratio of 41.5%. This is starting to get a bit aggressive, but nonetheless, based on her good credit and excellent employment history, the pre-approval was issued.

About a month goes by and I don't hear from Lucy. No big deal, I decided to give her a call and do what all good sales people do: stay in touch with our prospective clients. "Richard, I didn't buy a house yet but I'm about to buy a slick BMW roadster."

"Whoa," I said. "Do you know what that's going to do to your debt ratios?"

She didn't. Lucy assumed that once she was pre-approved to buy a home that her "pre-approval certificate" was good for 90 days and her debt ratios were a thing of the past. She didn't realize that any change to her financial picture could ruin her chance for home ownership. The payment on the BMW was $429/month.

$$\text{New BER} = \frac{\$2,691 + \$125 + 300 + \$429}{\$7,500} = \frac{\$3,545}{\$7,500} = 47.27\%$$

That's a high ratio! In fact, it is interesting to note that for the ratios to be exactly the same as before, Lucy would need to earn three times more than the car payment, or another $1,287 in monthly income, to offset the new debt. A raise was not in her immediate future. And if she would have bought the car, neither was a home. I insisted that the best thing she could do is to buy the house first, and then buy the car. Any dealership would grant you financing for a car after you own a house but the reverse definitely does not hold true. New house first, then new car!

In summation, debt can be a killer. If you find yourself with higher monthly obligations (student loans, credit cards, car payments, alimony), then you may have to postpone buying a home to get your financial house in order. Focus on paying off credit card debt. Swap out that expensive gym membership for a jump rope and an exercise ball. Brown bag-it to lunch and look on the internet for credit cards with lower interest rates to replace cards with higher rates. A little planning can end with a big reward.

One last thing about debt ratios: I used the classic number of 38% for the back-end debt ratio. Most banks will go to 42% on the back end and still approve the deal. Most senior level underwriters have the authority to sign off on back-end ratios of up to 50% but this is done by exception only. Regardless of the ratio, you have to live with the payments month in and month out including the taxes due twice a year and the home owners insurance premium. We'll talk more about this in the section entitled, "How Much House Can I Afford to Buy."

Down Payment and PMI

The easiest loan to obtain requires 20% down. With 20% down, banks do not require mortgage insurance, commonly called PMI. PMI is only one company that offers this insurance (like Kleenex) and you should know as insurance goes, it's not for your benefit - it's for the bank's. Homeowner's insurance rebuilds your house if there's a fire. PMI is an insurance premium that you pay monthly to **protect the bank** in the event that they have to foreclose on you. In the event of a foreclosure, the PMI company pays the bank a portion of the loan that is not recovered by the resale of your home to another buyer. Since PMI is willing to assume some of the risk, the bank is willing to make loans with as little as 3% down. If there weren't PMI companies, think how much longer it would take for people to save the 20% before they could afford to buy a house.

3% is the minimum you can put down on a conforming loan (loans under $417,000) and have just one loan. More recently, 0% down loans have been making a debut but these typically require two loans, usually an 80%, first and a 20%, second mortgage.

A second mortgage is just that. Loans are recorded chronologically and a second mortgage is a second loan that is recorded behind the first mortgage. In the event of foreclosure, the first mortgage gets paid off first and the second gets paid second. Being paid back second allows for the possibility of not being paid back at all. As such, these loans have more risk and therefore compensate that risk with a higher interest rate, which in effect makes your payments higher. On a good note, however, you just bought a home with 0% down.

FANNIE MAE recently introduced a true 100% financed, fixed rate loan. But this program is income capped and requires high credit scores. In other words, if you and/or your wife earn too much, or one of you has a low credit score, you will not qualify for this program. As of 2005, in Los Angeles, total household income cannot exceed $77,000. This dollar amount is set by Fannie May and varies by city and county.

Most people think the banks have it great. If a person doesn't pay for his mortgage, they can foreclose on a house, resell it and make all sorts of money. In reality, homes that have equity (current value less loan) usually get sold and the banks don't get them. Homes that have no equity, or worse, are upside down (the outstanding loans are greater than current value) are the homes banks usually end up getting back. That's why PMI is needed. The banks can afford to make a large loan on a home if someone else (PMI company) is willing to share the risk.

Contrary to popular belief, 3% down loans do not come with higher interest rates, just PMI. By law, once a home establishes that it has 21.5% in equity, lenders are required to drop the mortgage insurance premium.

Now, let's say you have 5% down and do not want to pay mortgage insurance because you heard the horror stories that you just can't get rid of it without doing a whole new refinance. Ask the lender if they have an 80% 1st mortgage and a 15% 2nd mortgage with you contributing 5% for the down payment. Since you have money vested in this deal, and assuming you have good credit, you will find that the 2nd mortgage in this scenario comes with a more attractive interest rate. And the easiest way to find out if this is a good deal is to have the lender do the math. Ask, "What are my payments with mortgage insurance vs. my payments with a 15% 2nd mortgage?" Take the program that has the lower payment unless you prefer to have just one payment a month since having a 2nd mortgage means sending in 2 checks, which is a minor inconvenience for perhaps significant savings.

Another advantage of having a 2nd mortgage is the fact that you can write off the interest that you pay on the 2nd mortgage. Mortgage insurance, on the other hand, is an insurance premium, often paid monthly, and unfortunately cannot be deducted for tax purposes. Also, make sure the same bank (lender) is writing both the 1st and the 2nd. It can get messy sometimes if different lenders are approving 2 different loans. Imagine having lender #1 approve you and lender #2 turning you down. This never happens when one lender approves both loans.

Employment

If you want to buy or refinance a house and you are like me, you're going to need a job. Some individuals can qualify based on interest income, dividends, royalties, or alimony income. But I don't have any of these, so I'm going to need a job.

So did Nancy Wilde. Nancy Wilde was a client of John Garland (no relation to Judy) of Southbay Brokers. John found her a beautiful little home: 2 bedrooms and 1 1/2 baths in the Torrance area of Los Angeles. Nancy worked for TRW in the Southbay area and had a solid income of $85,000 a year. She had a 60-day escrow and was fully approved. The appraisal was in, her supporting W-2's and paystubs confirmed her income, and her credit was great. There was one small problem - and one that you should be made aware. Two weeks before closing, the underwriter called to verify Nancy's employment. This is not an exception to the loan process. Verification of employment is often the last thing that gets done.

"Nancy no longer works here. Her last day was this past Friday. She left on commendable terms and we wish her well," said the Human Resource Representative.

"Thank you," replied the underwriter. The underwriter then notified the loan processor who notified the mortgage broker who notified John Garland that his deal was quickly flying south.

John quickly called his client. "What did you do that for? If you hated your job, why didn't you quit after we closed?"

"Why," asked Nancy? "I'll get another job. Do I really need one for this loan? I have the down payment and I have the savings."

Let me interject here, even though this wasn't my deal, "YES!! I mean, yes." It is important to show that you have an employment history and that you are gainfully employed during the loan process right through closing.

On a good note, it only took a week, but Nancy was able to find another job with a similar salary. The seller agreed to delay the closing of escrow for a week and John, not accustomed to making every escrow nerve racking, earned his commission.

In the mortgage industry, there are two types of people in the world: those who can document their income and those who can't. The latter are typically self-employed, take liberal tax write-offs and don't show enough income to qualify (per their tax returns). For these individuals, there are "Stated Income" programs.

Stated Income programs also known as low documented loans usually require that the borrowers have good credit and usually have more money to put down. Some companies will allow for 10% down, stated income programs, but a minimum credit score is required. I also know of one or two companies that will permit 0% down, low doc loans, with excellent credit scores assuming that the new mortgage payment does not exceed 150% of your current rent payment. If your rent is $1,000 per month then your new mortgage payment can't exceed $1,500 per month total, including taxes and insurance. With a Stated Income Program, the lender **does not require** the following:

- tax returns
- W2's
- pay stubs

They do require that your liquid assets are documented and will require the following:

- bank statements
- broker statements
- IRA's and 401K statements

The assumption is, that with a successful business, you are able to save enough money for the down payment and have enough reserves left over. Very often a bank will want to see at least 6 times your stated income in reserves in the bank. That way they know you run a profitable ship. But this is not a hard rule, and reserve requirements may vary with each lender.

Receiving a 100% gift from a relative for the down payment on this type of (low documented) loan is not acceptable. Again, that's because the assumption is that your business is successful and able to generate the down payment. If the gift is nonessential, then it's OK to receive it. Different lenders may permit a portion of the down to be a gift but this varies.

Since the lender is not documenting your income, there is naturally more risk associated with the transaction and yes, you can expect to pay a premium for this type of loan in terms of interest rate and/or fees, usually an 1/8% to a 1/4% in rate, especially with a fixed rate mortgage. There are adjustable products that require 20% down, and as such, do not charge more in rate. Again, this depends on the lender.

The Reiner's

Mr. and Mrs. John Reiner came to me to buy their next home. Mr. Reiner was a teacher for the L.A. Unified School District and worked in downtown Los Angeles. Mrs. Reiner received Social Security income of approx. $1,800 per month.

A nice feature of Social Security income is that many banks will allow this income to be grossed up by 25%. The assumption is that since taxes are not removed from Social Security and loan approvals are based on gross income (for W2 employees), that its acceptable to make the Social Security look like W2 income by grossing it up.

According to the Reiners, they wanted to apply for a low documented loan and not show their tax returns. That's because Mr. Reiner received additional income from tutoring, which either did not show up on the tax returns or showed up but was negated by expenses (write-offs).

Per Mr. Reiner, he made a gross income, including tutoring of $8,500, add his wife's income of social security (grossed up), they made $11,000 per month. The down payment for the new home, which cost $650,000, was coming from the proceeds of the sale of their old house. Other than these funds, the borrower did not have very much savings.

How does this deal sound to you? It's a low documented loan so the underwriter shouldn't be asking for tax returns. They have the down payment from the sale of their house, and the credit is fine. Slam dunk, right?

The underwriter called me. "Richard, where's their money?"

"Well, the down payment is coming from the sale of their house."

"No," said the underwriter. "Not where is their down payment, but where is their savings? How am I to believe that these individuals make $11,000 a month when they have very little savings? How am I to believe that they can afford to buy this home with significantly higher payments when they have very little savings accumulated? Shouldn't they have been able to save while living in their current home, having smaller payments from their smaller mortgage?" She had me.

She was right. While the Reiners claimed to be making a sizeable income, their profile simply did not support it. The client told me to write $11,000 so I did. But in a low doc loan the underwriter has the authority to say I don't believe it! In fact, they really have an obligation, on behalf of the bank, to not place the Reiners (buyers) in a financial situation that may end in foreclosure.

The Reiners were disappointed. When explaining the underwriter's point of view, they countered with the fact that Mr. Reiner will be taking on more classes to teach and more students to tutor to make up the shortfall. And that brings us to this conclusion: the profile that the underwriters are looking for is based on what you are currently earning, not what you think you may be earning. This was a big lesson for me. Remember Barry Kingston? Based on his savings the underwriter accepted the hole in his employment history and approved the deal. But for the Reiners, there wasn't a hole. There just wasn't any proof (based on their savings) that they could afford this home. And you know what? They will find a new house for a lower price and I guarantee they'll thank me.

A Fully Documented Loan is just that. You are either a W-2 employee or are self-employed, but show enough income to qualify. Be prepared to provide all of the above documents along with corporate or self-employed returns (1040's, 1120's, 1065's, K-1's), if applicable. Many lenders will be happy with just the two years of 1040's (federal returns).

John Ashly came to me after graduating from Harvard. His major was Art Appreciation and he recently landed a job with a local gallery here in Los Angeles that paid a base salary. In addition, he started an art auction business on the internet. Basically he would buy art and antiques from estate sales and then auction his newly acquired art on Ebay. The gallery job had a starting salary of $2,200 per month and he was confident that the auction business would easily bring in another $3,000 to $5,000 per month. The house he was looking to purchase was $500,000 and his dad was willing to give him a gift of $100,000 (nice dad).

Here's the rub. The gallery job is a W2 position. This income we can use even though he only had the job for 2 months. The bank will review his credit to make sure he has thus far been able to handle his financial obligations AND get a copy of his Harvard diploma. The diploma proves he completed what he said he completed. And he did. If the bank would have discovered that he lied about a diploma, the deal would have been dead. But that wasn't our issue.

When it comes to self-employed income, here's the problem: Banks want to see that you have been self-employed for a minimum of 2 years. Many require a 3-year history. My client, John Ashly, had only been doing it for 6 months. There's just no way for an underwriter to determine the viability of the company and therefore I couldn't use it.

Luckily, John Ashly belonged to a good family and his dad was able to co-sign with him. Co-signing can also be a tricky business, but the bottom line is that the person co-signing has to be able to contribute to the package. In other words, after the co-signer pays for his own living expenses plus his debt, he has to have enough discretionary income left over to be able to help you with your bills. John's dad was quite successful, so that is indeed what happened. The moral of the story, of course, is to make sure you are born into the right family.

Last thing: Regardless of being a W2 employee or self-employed, beware of tax "write-offs." "Write-offs," of course, are a great way of reducing your annual tax obligations but they are also a double-edge, sword. Have too many and you gladly may not have much income tax to pay… but you may also not qualify to buy a home. If you are a W2 employee, then your accountant will reveal the size of your write-off, probably on page 3 of your 1040 tax return. The actual form used is called a 2106. For self-employed, see your schedule "C." Your gross income, less expenses equals your net income and that's what's used for qualification purposes, not your gross income. Feel free to add back any depreciation you are writing off since this is typically a paper loss.

The Property Appraisal

For now, let's just say that if you are buying a home, the bank needs to agree that the house is worth what the contract sales price says it's worth. This typically is not a problem. After all, the value of a home is what you, the buyer and the seller agree to. Together, you constitute the market place. It's very unusual for an educated buyer, one who has been searching every Sunday for a home, to agree to pay more for a house than what it's worth. In other words, the market value of the house should be what other like homes in the area are selling for. The appraiser's job is to make sure that there are other similar homes in the area with similar sales prices. These like homes are called comparables and appraisers use a minimum of 3 other comps (comparables) to support (or not support) the purchase price.

When making an offer, your agent has access to the same information that the appraiser has and, in fact, his information is usually more current. Ask your agent to give you a map of the area and to identify like homes in the last six months that have sold in your prospective area. Let him explain to you why he feels this house is a good deal or at least reasonable. If the area lacks recent sales then it's acceptable for your agent (and the appraiser) to find comps in other similar neighborhoods. In these circumstances, you may want to drive this so-called similar neighborhood, to make sure that it's not a lot nicer, which may warrant a higher sales price.

In the section entitled "APPRAISAL" I'll discuss more about the mechanics of an appraisal and some of the standard appraisal theories. But for now, just know that the property has to appraise, and it's the last piece of the puzzle.

The Right Loan for the Right Home

Before we get specific about loan products, you need to answer these questions:

1) How long do I intend to keep the property?
2) Do I foresee interest rates going up or down?
3) Is my income steady and do I get commissions and/or bonuses?
4) How is my career outlook?
5) If married or soon to be married, does my spouse intend to work or stay at home?
6) Are we planning to have a family?

Jack and Betty Sue Forrester came to me to get pre-approved. The referral was from Bill Gardy of Southland Brokers. Jack was a bond trader and, if you are looking for a new profession, consider this one. In 4 years he went from about $45,000 in income to

$120,000 a year. Not bad for a new career. His last 2 years looked good. Betty Sue worked as a registered nurse and made about $50,000 a year. Their credit was fine. He had a mid credit score of 690 and hers was a very respectable 670. They were first-time homebuyers. To date, they had good incomes but they also had good spending habits. The house they were renting was for $2200 a month in Manhattan Beach and going out to dinner was very matter-of-fact.

"Jack, congratulations for jumping into the housing market," which is the beginning of my hope-you-work-with-me speech. "How long do you see yourself living in this house?"

"Well," started Jack. "This is our first home and it only has 2 bedrooms. My wife's currently pregnant with our first child, so I can't see us being here for more than 5 years."

(Mental note: Someone who is going to keep a house for 5 or less years probably doesn't need a fixed rate mortgage, especially since fixed are always priced higher than an adjustable and an adjustable offers terrific savings in both payments and less upfront points. The savings will be useful for the number of Pampers he's about to buy.)

"That's terrific," I said. "Congratulations again! Is your wife planning on working after she delivers?" This is a standard question but one many couples forget to discuss. Hopefully, they don't ask me for my opinion. If they do, they're going to hear about how important it is in child development for the mom to be around and that it's a good idea for you to consider buying a home on one income for the first 4 years, at least until the child is ready for preschool… assuming, of course, that they can afford to do this. Life offers plenty of challenges so I'm wise enough not to preach based on each individual's circumstances. I should tell you, however, plenty of my clients don't discuss this all-important issue. The result is always one very late-night, intense rap session.

"It's not definite, but we hope to make it on my salary."

(2nd mental note: Good for them. Now there's no need for me to count her income. Also, if her credit score was less then perfect, I could drop her from the application and improve their chance for getting approved. Regardless, it wasn't an issue for this couple. His income was strong and I'm assuming they already factored in that they would be looking for a less expensive house with one income.

A couple more questions and I'm ready to take the application.

"How's your career going? Bonds must have their ups and downs like the stock market. Are you concerned about your income disappearing?"

Jack explained that while the industry has its ups and downs, he does a very good job of growing his client base and is confident that any drop caused by a changing business cycle, will be offset by his ever-growing client base.

(3rd mental note: His job earns commissions and he has an increasing income track record. Whether you are commissioned or W2, if you feel confident that your earnings are increasing, then you can also feel confident that the risk associated with higher adjustable rates will be offset with your future higher earnings. Compare that to Jack's parents or others you may know on a fixed income. An adjustable rate for them could mean a future hardship if there are no other income sources to offset higher mortgage rates.

I asked them what loan they thought was best for them. While I thought an adjustable was right, nobody likes to be forced fed a loan. "My dad told me to get a fixed, that a fixed was most secure."

(4th mental note: Don't insult his dad.)

"Technically, your dad is right. It is the most secure. You never have to worry about it changing and going up. You know month-in and month-out how much to write the check for. At this time in the market place, with bond yields being so low (a fact he is very aware of), fixed rate loans are also more expensive."

I laid out some comparisons between the fixed and adjustables, and as he pointed out, reminded him that they weren't going to be in the house for more than 5 years. After looking at the initial dollars saved with lower points and the potential dollars saved over a

5-year period, he agreed. As such, I qualified them using the adjustable. And since these loans have lower interest rates, I was also able to qualify them for more home.

Just for the record, some banks/mortgage brokers will earn more commission if they sell one product vs. another. In my bank, they prefer loan consultants sell a bank product adjustable but we are not incented to do so. In this case, it just happened to be the right move.

If Jack had told me that his plan was to retain this property as a rental unit after 5 years then I might have concluded to sell the fixed. But for first-time home buyers who are going to need to buy washers, dryers, refrigerators, and a lot of pampers, take the savings.

Lastly, a lot of clients may make their decision regarding which rate to take based on what they think the economy is going to do. For instance, if you wanted to play world economist you might surmise that an improving economy would lead to higher inflation and that higher inflation rates always lead to higher mortgage rates. This is true ... but for as long as I have been doing this, I have never seen anyone predict *successfully* interest rate trends. Every time I think rates are going one way, a new jobs report comes out and interest rates do an about face. The moral of the story is, pick a loan product based on how long you expect to keep the house, is your income likely to increase or remain flat, and how much risk can you stomach. If a low adjustable rate mortgage means you save money but can't sleep at night for fear of higher rates, then get the fixed. It's your house and your loan. Get the product that makes you happy. Don't worry about the economy. It will take care of itself.

A Variety of Loans

The 30-year fixed. This loan is fully amortized over 30 years. In other words, if you keep this loan for 30 years both the interest and principal will be paid off in full. Every month, you will know exactly what to pay. That's comforting, as compared to an adjustable rate mortgage that is guaranteed to change. Many people assume that in the beginning of a mortgage that the payment is entirely interest. Not true. The amount of principal you pay off is small, but it's not 0. At todays' rates (6%), per $100,000, $102/month is your principal reduction on a $600 per month payment (approximately).

The 15-year fixed. This loan is fully amortized over 15 years. Since it pays off in half the time of a 30-year fixed, you might expect the payment to be twice as much. In truth, the monthly payment on a 15-year mortgage is about 30% more than a 30-year payment. This is great if you have a lot of income, not to mention, you'll save a fortune in accumulated interest. On the other hand, why get stuck having to make a bigger payment for 15 years? You can get a 30-year mortgage and accelerate the payments so that it pays off in 15 years. If your financial picture worsens, then you can always switch back to the lower 30-year payment and avoid a costly refinance.

You may be interested to know that 1 extra mortgage payment per year will reduce a 30-year mortgage to about 24.5 years.

Adjustable Rate Mortgages come in several flavors. Before we get into the particulars, there are a few terms that you need to be aware of. Know this and deciphering these loans will be…easier.

The basic formula is: The Index + The Margin = True Market Rate (or fully amortized rate).

The **True Market Rate** (also known as Fully Indexed Rate) is the rate that your mortgage payment is based on, assuming that this loan pays off in 30 years (as required). This number is guaranteed to change either monthly, semi-annually or annually based on the particular adjustable product you select and so will your payments.

The **Margin** is the spread that your lender charges, above the cost of borrowing the money. In other words, no matter what it costs the bank to borrow funds, the bank will always make a profit because of the margin. In general, banks love these loans. It guarantees them a profit for as long as this loan stays on their books.

The **Index** is the cost of borrowing the money. In other words, if the T-Bill (Treasury Bill) = 3%, the bank can borrow money from the Fed at 3%. If your margin = 2.50%, then your true market rate = 5.5% which is the actual rate at which your payment is based (index + margin). In this scenario, the 5.5% rate will change and you will have to pay the new rate if the loan is to payoff in 30 years.

The **Teaser Rate** – This is the big bold advertised rate that sucks you in. "Buy Today: 1.95% Start Rate". It's too good not to call! In reality, however, you get this rate for a small amount of time, often 1 to 3 months, and then it can change monthly. Or, you get to keep the rate for the whole year but can accrue deferred interest (see Negative Amortized Loans, below).

Lifetime Caps are the maximum rate an adjustable rate mortgage can go. Currently, a majority of life caps are approximately 10.95%. This is the highest your rate can ever go (before you pass out).

Prepayment Penalties are often offered with adjustable rate mortgages. I don't favor them because they lock you into a loan. In other words, if you take a loan with a prepayment penalty, you will have to pay thousands of dollars to get out of your loan, usually between 1 to 5 years. Obviously, the shorter term penalty is preferred (1 year) if you have to take one. Some companies do offer what they call **"soft prepays"** which means if you go back to your original lender for refinancing or for a new purchase money loan, they will waive the penalty. Be careful! These loan add-ons can show up on the unsuspecting. Prepayment penalties are used by lenders to add some very attractive features to their loans, and they may be worth it if you are sure you are not going to change your mind and want a lower refinanced rate in one year should rates drop. For instance, many companies will reduce their lifetime cap by 2% if you take a 3-year prepay. That means that a 11.95% life cap can be dropped to 9.95%. If you favor adjustables, that's terrific, although it's extremely doubtful that the rate would get that high in three years anyway. My advice is, if you have to take a prepay penalty, make sure you get an immediate benefit (i.e., 0 points or lower margin).

A Mrs. Lorenzo came to me and wanted a 5-year loan (see Hybrid Loans below). That's a loan that is fixed for 5 years and becomes an adjustable thereafter. This product's rate is always lower than a fixed rate mortgage on any given day and they are very popular.

Her loan was for $525,000 and the rate was 5.375% with 0 points. At the time, the jumbo fixed rate at 0 pts. was over 6.25%. And to make it even more attractive, my bank offered a .25% interest rate discount if you accepted a 3-year prepayment penalty. Simply put, that meant that she could not refinance or sell her property for 3 years without incurring a 2% penalty. 2% is significant. On a $525,000 loan, that's a penalty of $10,500. That's not chump change!

On the flip side, a .25% reduction in the interest rate equaled a monthly savings of $81 per month which is a savings of approximately $1,000 per year just for accepting a prepay penalty feature on your loan. That's nothing to sneeze at either.

I remember our conversation. "Richard, which would you do?"

"Mrs. Lorenzo," I started. "You just bought the house, the rates are incredibly low, you don't plan on moving, I would take the $81 in monthly savings. After all, rates are at a 30-year low and how much lower can they go?" Those words, "How low can they go," will soon haunt me.

Mrs. Lorenzo agreed with my advice and took the loan with the prepayment penalty.

About 6 months ago, I got a phone call. "Richard, this is Mrs. Lorenzo. I want to refinance. Your bank is now offering 5-year money at 4.375%! Since I am refinancing with you and the same bank, I do not expect to be held responsible for that prepayment penalty that you insisted I take."

"Oy." I re-explained all of the reasons why we did what we did at the time but it was no good. I was now the evil loan officer that duped her into a bad situation. "Mrs. Lorenzo, you can't get out of the penalty. The bank's policy is that they will not waive a prepayment penalty for hell or high water. You just have to wait for your 3 years to be up." Her response? *(Click.)*

The bottom line is, I no longer suggest that anyone take a prepayment penalty. They do have benefits: potential lower rates, lower life caps, lower margins. But you won't be taking this feature as one of my suggestions.

Finally, when it comes to adjustables, always shop index and margin. You want a stable index, one that moves slowly, and obviously the lower the margin the better. Forget the teaser rate. These typically disappear quickly. The lower the margin, the lower the payment. Indexes can change monthly, semi-annually, or annually. Personally, I like the 12 MAT (Monthly Average Treasury). This index is averaged over 12 months, which causes it to move very, very slowly. The COFI (Cost of Funds Index) is a 4-month average and used to be very popular. It appears that the COFI products are being replaced by the 12 MAT in the industry.

Hybrid Loans – These loans have initial interest rates that are fixed for a predetermined length of time and then roll into adjustables for the remainder of the term. Their name often identifies their fixed portion, such as, the 3/1, 5/1, 7/1, and 10/1 Adjustable Rate Mortgage (ARM's). The 3/1 is fixed for 3 years, the 5/1 for 5 years, etc. The 1 of the 5/1 implies that this loan will adjust once a year, every year after the 5 year period for the remaining 25 years. During its adjustable period, the rate can not go up or down by more than 2 percent per year, tied to T-bills, and has a lifetime cap typically of 5 or 6% over the start rate (i.e., if the fixed portion is at 6.25%, then the life cap will be 11.25%. These loans offer an opportunity to save on an interest rate that is always lower than the 30-year fixed rate. They are perfect if you feel confident that a move up is in your future or if you just need lower payments while you get your feet planted. You can always refinance down the road.

The savings can be quite significant for these loans when compared to a 30-year fixed.

Do the exercise and compare for your self. Calculate the monthly payments for both the 30-year fixed and, say, the 5/1 ARM. Subtract the two monthly payments and multiply by 60 months. The savings can be substantial. In my opinion, if you think you are going to move up, or refi, or job relocate, or need the extra cash, give this loan serious consideration. The savings can make this loan a winner.

Hybrid loans – Interest Only. Like the other hybrid loans, these products are fixed for the initial period. Unlike the hybrid loans identified above, these loans allow for interest-only payments. As a result, it is possible to make payments for several years and never pay down the initial loan balance. That makes for low payments! In addition, if you choose to make a payment in excess of the minimum payment required, your principal balance is reduced. This loan is terrific for people who are self-employed, earn commission income and/or bonus income. They can have low payments throughout the year while their income is low and gain equity through larger payments when their commissions and bonuses kick in. It's probably my favorite loan due to flexibility.

Negative Amortized Loans - The trickiest loan to understand and the most aggressive loan product.

These loans are characterized by their unusually low start rate and their **three payment options**. The best way to explain this product is by example.

Loan Amount = $300,000

Start rate (Teaser)	Index	Margin	Initial Paym't	Int.only Paym't	Fully Indexed Paym't (5.5%)
2.95%	3.0	2.50	$1,256	$1,375	$1,703

Option 1

For this particular loan, you can pay the below market interest rate (Teaser Rate) of 2.95% ($1,256/mo) for a full year. After that time, **the payment, not the interest rate**, will increase by 7.50% (industry standard). So, in year 2 your new payment will be $1,350/month ($1,256 x 107.5%). In year 3 it will be $1,451/month ($1,350 x 107.5%), and so on. These year to year increases can go on typically for 5 years. So far so good, right?

Option 2

This option allows for interest only payments. The rate is based on the index plus the margin. You can pay $1,375 a month or however much it is each month as the index changes. Your principal balance will not go down ever but, then again, if the value of your property is appreciating, then who cares?

Here's where it gets tricky: The difference between the artificially low payment of $1,256 and the interest only payment of $1,375 equals $119. This is called **The**

Negative or is referred to as **Deferred Interest**. This is the amount **each month** THAT YOUR PRINCIPAL BALANCE WILL RISE BY. Did you get that? Rather than gaining equity, you are losing equity! When not explained properly, borrowers have a tendency to pass out when they find out that they owe more money on their mortgage today than when they bought the house 5 years ago. In other words, negative amortization means negative equity.

Oh, did I mention I love this loan? I do. Again, it gives you an opportunity to own more house than you can normally afford and, as long as you pay back the negative with bonus checks or commission checks, you'll never get into trouble.

Option 3

Pay the Fully Indexed Payment and never get into trouble. This payment ($1,703/month) will also change monthly, and is comprised of both interest and principal. Or, on slow income earning months, pay the minimum and on good income earning months pay the fully indexed payment. It's your choice. As you can truly see, this is really the most aggressive loan available today.

One more thing: This is a loan that many banks offer with either a 30- or 40-year term. That means it has to be paid off in that time. To make sure you do not get into too much trouble, the bank will **RECAST** your loan if the principal balance reaches 110% of the original balance. RECAST means to recalculate your payments so that eventually you will have to pay both principal and interest so that the loan pays off as required. If you go through the exercise in Option 1, that usually takes place in about year 5 if you consitantly choose to go negative.

Here are some other advantages to this loan. If you know your income will be higher next year than this year, why not defer all of the negative interest to next year when you can use the tax write-off? Writers, attorneys settling large cases, CEOs receiving a large bonus, individuals who know they are going to sell stock options next year, can all have a better tax write-off when they need it. As you can see, this can be a terrific loan as long as you understand how it works.

Adjustables – non negative. These loans are typically tied to T-Bills and have a 2.75 margin. They usually move 1% per 6 months or 2% per year. They do not have a negative option. They start off low and their teaser rate has more value since it lasts for a while. Personally, I prefer the Neg-Am. loans. They are more flexible in payments and usually come with lower margins.

Indexes

1 Year T-Bill – Weekly average of the U.S. Treasury with a constant maturity of 1 year.

12 MAT – Monthly Average Treasury - a 12-month average of the U.S. Treasury with a constant maturity of 1 year. This index moves much slower due to the effects of averaging.

11ᵗʰ District – The 11ᵗʰ District designates the west coast to the Federal Reserve. This is an average of the interest rates that are paid to bank customers as well as what the Fed charges its member banks to borrow funds. Its rates are also averaged, typically over 4 months, and are also very slow moving. This index is becoming less popular as more lenders are switching to the 12 MAT.

LIBOR – London Interbank Offer Rate – This is a European prime rate. It can be very low depending upon the economic health of our friends abroad. When it moves, however, it moves fast, much like our prime rate in the U.S.

Interest Rates vs. Points vs. A.P.R.

The APR, or Annual Percentage Rate, as it is affectionately called is not the rate from which your monthly payments are based. The APR is a number that each company calculates for the rate you select. It includes the simple interest rate, the bank's fees to obtain your loan, and 15 or 30 days of prepaid mortgage interest all rolled up into one number that you can use as a comparison tool. In other words, rather than call up lender "A" and ask for their rate, discount points, origination fee, appraisal fee, underwriting fee, etc., you can simply ask what is your APR. Just think how much faster your phone calls can be when trying to find a good rate. Unfortunately, different banks include different things in their APR, which may influence this number. For example, some banks include 15 days of prepaid interest while others include 30 days (see Tricks of the Trade).

If you want to use APR as a comparison tool, ask banks to quote their APR based on a specific rate (say 7.0 %) and for a 30- or 60-day interest rate lock. This will get you closer to a reliable tool.

Harvey and Susan Hunter came to me in search of a low fixed rate loan. They had an accepted offer on their new purchase and asked me if I could quote them our current 30-year rate. Some bank managers would prefer that the sales force not quote rate, as it is apparent that many clients are just shopping and would quickly get off the phone, leaving little chance of making the deal. I don't mind. A conversation has to start somewhere so it may as well start with rate.

"Our current rate is 6.5% with 1 point," I told them.

"Oh, too bad," they responded. "We'd like to go with you since you work for our bank but we were quoted 6.375% with another lender."

"How many points," I asked.

The answer was 1.50 points. So, the question becomes which is the better deal. After all, the rate is an 1/8th lower but the cost is a 1/2 point more.

Let's do a comparison. Which is truly lower?

A 30-year Fixed with an interest rate of 6.50% with 1 point or

A 30-year Fixed with an interest rate of 6.375% with 1.5 points.

(Points represent a percentage of the loan balance. 1 point = 1%. 1.5 points = 1.5% of the loan).

Assuming a $200,000 loan, let's do the math:

Rate	6.50%	6.375%	Difference
Points in $	$2,000	$3,000	$1,000 at the close of escrow
Monthly Payment	$1,264.14	1,247.73/mo	$16.40/ month

So in this example what is the better loan? The quickest answer may be, do the Hunters have the extra $1,000 to spend at closing? If the answer is "no," then 6.50% is definitely the better deal.

Suppose they do have an extra $1,000. Then, the best way to answer this question is to make it a function of time. At what point do the Hunters make up the $1,000 they spent at closing, with their long-term monthly savings of $16.40 per month.

$1,000 / 16.40 = 60.91 months or 5 years.

In other words, the Hunters should spend the extra grand at closing if they are sure that they will live in the home for more than 5 years. If their plan is to move within 5 years, then the better deal is to take the higher rate.

Looking at loans in terms of how long you will live there is always a better way to approach this problem, not just for which rate is better, but for which loan product is better as well.

When shopping rates and points always hold one or the other constant. In other words, when calling several lenders always ask, "What are your points and fees for a 6.50% interest rate?" Or, "what is your rate on a 30-year fixed for 1.5 points?" The reason is that very low interest rates and very high interest rates are always available. It is really just a question of how many points it costs to buy a particular rate. In our above example, it so happens that an 1/8 in interest rate can be purchased for one half point from most lenders. Thus, in regards to the Hunters, I also could have quoted 6.375% for 1.50 points. That's why when you shop, you need to choose several constants: rate or points, and loan product (i.e., 30-year fixed).

For the record, it is actually easier to make the interest rate the constant. A lender may not have a 1% point option. A particular rate may cost .875 points or 1.125 points. Hence, they may not have a 1-point quote. If you select the rate, however, the respective number of points can be quoted.

Lastly, and complicating the issue, rates change daily. So if you call Lender "A" on Monday and Lender "B" on Tuesday, you can't make a fair comparison. The rate from each lender may have been the same on the same day. Furthermore, how long is your escrow period? Typically, the longer the escrow period, the more you will have to pay in incremental points to lock in a rate. The difference in dollars can be as much as a quarter point (.25%) for a 60-day rate lock assuming a 60-day escrow period versus a 30-day escrow period. Locking the interest rate means that the rate will not fluctuate during the escrow period.

Good Faith Estimate

The best way to get an interest rate quote from a lender is to ask them to fax you a Good Faith Estimate for a locked rate for the escrow period you need.

The Good Faith Estimate will identify the rate the lender can lock **that day** and their fees as well as fees from 3rd party vendors (escrow, title, etc.). While 3rd party vendor fees are indeed estimates, the fees charged by the lender should not change, except possibly the appraisal fee. Appraisal fees will vary depending upon complexity, number of units, loan size and whether it's a full or drive-by appraisal.

Once you receive competing faxes, you should be in a much better position to make an educated decision about which lender you'd like to choose. However, make sure you like the guy/woman on the other line. He/she is responsible for your entire loan experience and getting you the right loan for your new home.

Personally, I would gladly sacrifice an 1/8th in rate if it means I can trust the person I am dealing with and don't have any last minute blood-pressure-raising, vein-popping, stress-inducing excuses that delay or threaten the closing of my new home.

Here's a list of typical fees charged by the lender:

Points = A percentage of your loan balance as related to your interest rate.

Tax Service fee - $81 (a tax reporting agency that notifies your lender if you stop paying property taxes).

Credit report - $10 per report pulled.

Wire charge - $35 (cost of wiring funds from the bank to the title co. (escrow).

Flood Certificate - $18 (a 1 page report indicating if your new home is in a flood zone). Appraisal fee – $325 (an interior report certifying value).

Underwriting and review fee* - $430. (can have different names but this is what the bank collects to offset the cost of processing your loan).

*Other names of fees that lenders may charge, but are really just dollars collected to either offset costs, or for additional profit, are called: Processing fee, Underwriting fee, Document Preparation fee and Review fee.

How Much House Can I Afford?

There are a couple of ways to answer this question, but the truth is there's only one good answer: How much are you comfortable paying?

It used to be that the banks allowed you to buy a home with a housing payment equal to 1/3 of your gross income. If you (and your spouse) earned $6,000 per month, then the bank allowed you to buy a home with a total housing payment of $2,000 per month. Taxes and insurance take up approximately 20% of the payment ($400/month). In other words, based on a $6,000 per month income, you can afford principal and interest payments of $1,600 per month ($2,000 - $400). Using a financial calculator (or the chart at the back of this book), you would qualify for a loan amount of $218,000. Add a 10% down payment (divide 218K by .90) and your sales price = $242,000.

That's the way it was. In the competitive environment we live today, many of the old rules went out the window and many lenders will qualify you for a lot more home based on your particular circumstances.

A better way to approach this subject is to figure out what is the maximum payment that you are comfortable making on a monthly basis. To compensate for the tax advantages of owning a home, add approximately 30% to your maximum payment since this represents the tax benefit that you will get back from Uncle Sam (see Tax Advantages).

To increase any number by 30%, divide that number by the complement (.70).

i.e., 2,000/.7 = 2,857. ($2,857 is exactly 30% more than $2,000). Talk to your accountant to confirm your particular tax rate, which will be substituted in line 2 below.

Here's the formula for determining how much home you should buy in a linear format:

1) Determine a comfortable payment.

2) Add 30% to that payment (by dividing by .70) to compensate for tax savings.

3) If you are making a 20% down payment, multiply this new number by .78 to factor out taxes and insurance (which = approximately 22%). Less than 20% down, multiple by .76.

4) This number represents your true comfortable payment after tax savings and takes into account your monthly tax and monthly insurance obligation.

5) Use this number at the back of this book to determine how much loan at current interest rates you can afford to buy.

6) Add your down payment to the loan amount to determine your sales price. Divide by .95

for a 5% down payment, by .90 for a 10% down payment, etc.

There are plenty of sites on the internet that will also tell you how much house you can afford to buy. You might check out www.askjeeves.com (plug in the word "amortization"), www.bankrate.com or www.wamumortgage.com Any of these sites do a nice job of telling you how much you can afford based on your monthly income and monthly expenses. Unfortunately, like the old rules, these sites are often too conservative. They will qualify you using ratios of 28 over 36, which is atypical for borrowers qualifying in Southern California where housing prices are a lot higher than the rest of the country. Most underwriters recognize this and qualify people for a lot more. That's why qualifying based on your comfort level works better than plugging in your gross income on these automated systems. Then again, the Internet is quick and fun and it can't hurt for a starting point. Just know that you will qualify for more, which will be apparent after you speak to a mortgage professional.

Or determine your comfortable monthly payment and call a mortgage professional. Any one of them will be happy to tell you the appropriate sales price and ask if you'd like to get pre-approved/approved right away.

Here are a couple of misconceptions that need to be corrected:

1) I want to put the least amount down so I can have the biggest loan for a tax write-off.

Truth – Check with your accountant, but typically you have to spend at least $3 in mortgage-interest payments to get $1 back in tax savings - not a great way to grow rich.

2) I need to put down 20% to avoid mortgage insurance.

Truth – That used to be true, but today you can get a convenient 2nd mortgage to help with the down payment. These loans are called 80, 10 and 10's or 80, 15 and 5's (80 1st mortgage, 15% 2nd mortgage and 5% down). Then again, mortgage insurance isn't that bad and I wouldn't let it bother you.

3) If you have excellent credit, you don't need to have a down payment. You can finance 100% of the sales price.

Truth – This is true. But it is also true that you are going to pay a higher interest rate than individuals with at least 3% down for conforming loans and 5% down for jumbo loans. Usually, a 100% financed loan is made up of two loans, an 80% first mortgage, and a 20% second mortgage. While the rate on the first mortgage may be competitive, the interest rates on the second are typically a lot more expensive.

And the biggest truth of all is that individuals with good credit and savings will have an opportunity to get the best prevailing interest rates in the market place.

A Word or Two About Rates

They move. Typically, they move daily, usually once a day in the morning. On a turbulent day on Wall Street, they can move more than once a day, but usually it is just once.

In general, it works like this: If the economy is doing well, you can expect to see mortgage rates go higher. If it appears that the economy is headed toward a recession, you can expect to see rates go lower. Fear of inflation, strong manufacturing, low unemployment and strong consumer confidence are all signs of an improving economy (except maybe inflation) and point towards higher rates. The opposite holds true for falling rates.

The ever-popular 30-year fixed rate mortgage is based on the 10-year bond, not the 30-year bell weather bond. That's because most people keep their home or their mortgage no more than 9 to 11 years on average. To view the movement of the 10-year bond, you can go to any popular financial web site or look at the front page of the LA Times business section. At the bottom of the page is the 10-year, bond yield. As the yield goes up, so do fixed mortgage rates...in general. It is not a hard and fast rule since mortgages really track mortgage-backed securities but they do seem to move in the same direction. Here are some of the sites I like to check out:

www.cnnmoney.com or www.Bondtalk.com or www. yahoo.com (fianance tab)

All are updated through out the day and should give you a good indication of which way rates are moving. Bond Talk tells you today's yields, yesterday's yields, last week's yields, and last month's yields. If you like to play economist, go ahead. If there's a prevailing trend, you may see it here. There's a lot more information on this screen than you need but just look at the bond yields you need (10-year for 30-year fixed, 5-year for 5-year adjustables).

The company I work for prices our rates every day at 7 a.m. on the West Coast. That means the bond market has been open on the East Coast for only an hour and a half. In that time, the Pricing Department has the responsibility of deciding what the rates are going to be, implementing all changes into the rate sheets, and faxing this info throughout the country. I was very surprised that they could do it in an hour. I asked head of pricing how it could be done so quickly! His response: due to time constraint, they hardly look at the U.S. bond market for that day. Instead, they look at yesterday's activity, then Tokyo and London. They track equity and bond markets right around the globe. The next morning, they'll take a quick glance at our markets and make their decisions.

First Time Home Buyer Programs

Suzanne Gifford came to me in the summer of 2003. She had been renting for some time and felt good about her financial outlook. She and her husband Jim had been at their current jobs for over 3 years now and were making a decent living. Jim had his own company in promotional merchandising, company mugs, pens, key chains, etc., and Suzanne had some seniority as a cashier at a local supermarket. She proudly stated that they were first-time buyers and was very aware that there were programs just for them. Our conversation, and her shock went something like this:

"My husband and I have been paying over $1,400 per month in rent. We feel confident we can easily afford that, or another $400 more and can own something. As a first-time buyer, do you have a program with 0 percent down?

I began, "Right now, we require a minimum of 3% down. On a good note, however, that can come as a gift. Do you have the savings or do you know of a relative that can give you a gift?"

"I don't know," she said. "I can ask our parents but I'll have to look into that, what about your interest rates. As a first-time buyer, are we entitled to a lower rate?"

"Actually, the rates for first-time buyers are often slightly higher, but not always. Typically, the FHA (Government insured) rates are slightly higher. We'd have to look into which program is right for you."

"But as first-time buyers, lenders are suppose to be more lenient. Jim is self-employed and he takes a lot of 'write-offs' for our taxes. We've had no problem paying our rent so there's no need to review our tax returns, is there?"

"Yes," I said (hesitantly). "Without a minimum of 10% down I'd have to review 2 years of your tax returns to determine if you show enough income to qualify."

"I don't believe this! Why do they promote first-time buyer programs if they are harder to qualify?"

Perhaps I should have begun my conversation with Suzanne with a pop quiz:

Suzanne, first-time buyer programs are terrific because:

a) They offer you lower interest rates.
b) They charge less points (fees).
c) The bank qualifies you regardless of your income.
d) None of the above.

She would have surely selected "a", "b", and "c", while the correct answer is "d".

Many people make this mistake. They feel that as a first-time home-buyer you deserve a reward for jumping into the home ownership market. Mind you, Suzanne and her husband do not have any experience making mortgage payments and like many, there's a good chance that they will not be putting a lot down. Most lenders see this as additional risk, as in, there's a higher chance of your letting a home go into foreclosure then say someone with a track record of owning a home for some time. More risk means that the lender will want to be compensated for that risk in the form of higher interest rates or higher fees. Not always, but it does happen.

So where's the benefit? Why declare a program if it's more costly to the buyer? Here are the reasons in no particular order:

Low Down Payment – Banks typically will make loans up to $417,000 (conforming loan limit) with as little as 3% down. That 3%, however, has to be from your savings. It can't be a gift, and it can't suddenly show up one day. This is a Fannie Mae/Freddie Mac requirement. You need to be able to show that it's been there for at least 2 months. That means that it has to be there for 3 months in order to show a 2-month average balance. Now the good news: Several first-time buyer programs allow for the entire 3% to come as a gift from a relative (not a friend). And coming soon, 0 % down programs will be made available for first-time buyers. Zero down payments will definitely require a good credit history.

Easier credit – As we mentioned earlier, having good credit is king. First-time buyer programs are a little more lenient on credit. They rely less on your credit score and more on reasonable explanations as to why you may have been late regarding your financial obligations at one time or another. Lates on a credit report due to a medical condition at one time during an illness is much more acceptable then periodic 'lates' on a Ford Mustang.

Down payment assistance – Also known as silent seconds. Many cities have assistance programs that give you the down payment if you buy your home in a particular census tract. This down payment is recorded as a second lien behind the first mortgage. This is not acceptable on any other loan except a first-time buyer program if it's defined in the loan program's guidelines.

Seller Contributions – Most loans allow for a seller to pay for the buyer's non-recurring closing costs if you can work that into your purchase contract. Non-recurring closing costs are costs that do not reoccur, also known as one-time fees. Examples are: the escrow fee, title fee and bank fees (points, processing fee, etc). Several first-time buyer programs allow for the seller to pay for both non-recurring, as well as recurring closing costs. Examples of recurring fees are property taxes, mortgage payments and property insurance. As you can see, this feature makes it a lot less expensive for first-time buyers to buy their first home.

Non-occupant Co-Borrower Income – Many applicants assume that if they **cannot** income qualify on their own, that they can get a parent to co-sign. By adding Dad's income, surely their debt ratios will look a lot better. Not so fast! Most lenders want the borrower who is going to live in the property to be able to qualify on his own. Having a non-occupying co-signer will allow the Underwriters to be a little more aggressive when qualifying you, but you still have to pretty much qualify on your own without dad's income. Some first-time home buyer programs (especially FHA insured loans), however, will allow for debt ratio qualifying with both incomes. This can be a major advantage, especially for those individuals that are self-employed and do not show much income.

I do not know of any first-time buyer programs that allow for "Low Doc" or "Stated Income" programs. You will need to show W-2s and pay stubs or two years of tax returns to support your income if any of the above circumstances apply to you.

In summation, being a first-time buyer does not mean that you have to apply for a first-time buyer program. These programs are available to help those individuals that have special circumstances as identified above. If these circumstances do not apply to you, then you are probably better off avoiding them as they can be slightly more expensive.

Tricks of the Trade

Bait-and-Switch – This seems to be one of those catch-all phrases for customers that come to the realization that they were lied to. Examples would be:

- They said my rate is 6.25% but the loan doc's say 6.375%.

- The points are supposed to be .50%, not 1.50%.
- I was told I was getting a fixed-rate mortgage. This is an adjustable.
- I'm happy that the points are 0 but the fees are very high.
- I was told there were 0 points. What's this 1.0% origination fee (points with a unique name)?
- Yeah it's a great rate but he never mentioned a prepayment penalty.

Basically, you are promised the world so that the broker has one more deal in his pipeline. Then, one week before closing, you are in for a surprise. And since you really don't have enough time to find and get reapproved for a new loan, you will take this one. The mortgage broker will apologize for making an error and insist that you look at the big picture, "You got the home." Disgruntled, but determined to close on time (per your contract), you close. Sometimes, their mistakes are honest, and a lot of times they'll say whatever they need to in order to get the deal. You were swayed by his promise of a better rate, his superior service and that he shopped hundreds of lenders.

What about the promise that they shop hundreds of lenders? Doubtful. Most mortgage brokers send their deals to a couple of lenders, which is fine. There are some investors (lenders), however, that will pay a bigger commission to the broker if he sends the loan package to them. In these cases, the mortgage professional (so called) has a bigger interest in his wallet rather than in yours.

In regard to brokers having the best rates, this is debatable. In today's marketplace it's a very competitive business. In fact, in regard to a conforming (<$417,000) 15- or 30-year fixed-rate mortgage, all lenders (and brokers) get their money (to lend) from Fannie Mae and Freddie Mac. Since they buy it from the same source, they can offer it for the same price, give or take the fees it costs to process your loan. Since the rates will be similar, my advice is to shop service. The rate will not be "far superior" as they pitched. If it is, WATCH FEES. Some lenders/brokers offer a better rate only to be compensated in higher fees. Remember our interest rate comparison between 6.375% and 6.50%? A 1/2 point in fees ($) can buy an 1/8 in rate. Thus, if the broker's points are the same but their rate is an 1/8 better, make sure they didn't bury 1/2 point in fees somewhere.

The nice thing about working for a direct lender is that not only do they have very competitive rates, but they only need to know (by heart) their lending guidelines, and that can be challenging enough. As such, it's my belief that an experienced direct lender will be more accurate more often about the loan that is right for you. True mortgage brokers need to know everyone's guidelines and that's a pretty tall order, which can get them into trouble.

A favorite way for brokers and a lot of bank lenders to earn a bigger commission is by playing the market. The client chooses to "float" his rate during the application process. **"Floating"** means not locking the interest rate, which can change daily, on the assumption that everyone thinks it's going to go lower. Of course, if rates improve during the next 30 days, then the client should get the best rate that day. Unfortunately, some brokers/lenders will pass the better rates to their clients, and some will give a better rate, just not the best rate. By selling a slightly higher rate, the broker again receives additional compensation (commission). The best way to avoid this is by locking your rate at the time of application and by not giving the broker the opportunity to play games. By the way, this goes for some lenders also. Brokers are not the only ones who can benefit this way.

You might ask how mortgage professionals are paid. In general, buried in the interest rate is an earned commission to the broker/loan officer. In other words, if I make a loan at 6.0% for 0 points, how am I paid? After all, the lender is not charging any points to pay my commission. Well, the bank (and industry) has built my commission into the rate. This is great for both the loan officer/broker and the buyer. But here's where it gets tricky. There are ways to earn additional commission, some of which are not to the buyer's advantage. Here's a list of features to look out for. Sometimes they are necessary, and sometimes they are added to spike a commission check.

- The margin on an adjustable rate mortgage seems a little high. This will cost you each month and earns a broker a bigger check.

- A 3- to 5-year prepayment penalty added to your loan. Prepays can sometimes lower your rate, and again they can reward the mortgage professional. They are, however, required often on some 0 point loans.

- An adjustable with a higher start rate is one way to earn a bigger check but usually the kicker is in the margin.

The inflated commission comes back to the broker in the form of a rebate. As such, this policy is called rebate pricing. Rebate pricing says that if the broker sells any of these features above the normal rates, then the broker is entitled to additional compensation. In other words, you pay more in the form of a higher rate and the broker gets paid more. You might think this is crooked. In my opinion, sometimes it is. If you have "A" credit and are getting a decent size loan, I don't see why you should pay a premium to the broker.

There are times, however, where it is justified: on small loans or on loans that are difficult to process or on loans that will take a long time to process due to their level of difficulty. If a mortgage broker/loan officer is not adequately compensated for his effort, he or she will simply stop working on these (small or difficult) loans. Then the real injustice will be a certain percentage of the public that wants to buy a house but can't find a lender to help them. That's why Congress has not ruled against these kinds of rebates or pricing strategies. The entire public, regardless of age, lack of wealth or ethnic background needs to have access to home ownership and mortgage professionals need to be adequately compensated, but not overly compensated.

What about the broker/lender who suggests not locking your interest rate until after the Fed meets next week to discuss monetary policy? The Fed refers to the Federal Reserve. They typically meet once a month to discuss whether or not to adjust the interest rate on the Federal Funds Rate. This is the interest rate that banks use to borrow money from the Federal Reserve or from each other, NOT the 30-year fixed rates. Nonetheless it does set the tone for the market and does impact long-term interest rates. Unfortunately, even if the Fed lowers the Fed Funds Rate, there is no guarantee that long-term rates (30-year) follow. In fact, I have seen just the opposite happen. The Fed lowers rates and 30-year fixed rates go up! The bottom line is that if your broker/lender is such an expert in the bond market, why isn't he a bond trader. He or she should be a millionaire by now! To be fair, however, I'm sure they are right 50% of the time.

Whether you apply with a broker, a direct lender or a mortgage banker, you should lock the rate from Day One and make sure that the lender has a **"Float Down"** **policy**. A Float Down policy says that if mortgage rates improve during the application process, that your lender has a product feature that allows them to offer you a lower rate prior to closing. Now you've got your cake and you can eat it to! By insisting that you want a locked rate from Day One with a Float Down policy, the broker has to quote his most competitive rate he has, provide a Good Faith Estimate of closing costs and has **less of an opportunity** to play around with your loan. And if rates improve, your rate will improve too.

Not all lenders have "float down" policies. Some companies insist that once you lock, that's it. They will not give you a lower rate. The broker might insist that he can always go to another lender and get you a lower rate. That's not happening! Once your loan has been processed and you are a couple of weeks from closing, neither you nor the broker are going to want to chance having your loan reprocessed at a new lender where it can be declined or miss your closing contract date due to the time needed to rework your loan.

Have I been a little harsh about mortgage brokers? This isn't to say that all mortgage brokers are bad. There are a lot of good ones out there that are honest, hard working and do a great job for their clients. And in some cases, they are the best resource for getting a new home loan. If one of the following situations applies to you then a mortgage broker may be in your future:

- You have bad credit.
- You had a bankruptcy/foreclosure in the last three years.

- You do not have any funds for a down payment.
- You need a co-signer for a jumbo loan (loans greater than $417,000).
- You have a significant down payment, bad credit, and can't show tax returns.

For these people, a mortgage broker does have multiple lenders that he can pursue. And in these situations, brokers are definitely the heroes.

It turns out that one of the best tricks of the trade was unintentional. It's the APR (Annual Percentage Rate). By law, all mortgage professionals are suppose to quote and disclose their APR's. This is the one number that combines all of the costs associated with the transaction. So, companies often quote low APRs and forget to mention the points. It's a great way to get the phone to ring! A low APR may sound terrific until you get the Good Faith Estimate, which identifies that you are paying 2.50 points for this loan. Sure the rate is low but your costs are very high since 2.5 points equals 2.5% of your loan balance! When shopping for a loan, the APR may be a good place to start, but make sure you get a written Good Faith Estimate to layout the lender's fees.

As when buying anything, let the buyer beware. You should always ask the right questions - and don't be afraid to shop around. Only by asking a lot of specific questions can you insure that you are being taken care of and getting the best deal for your money. Rate's important, but not as important as finding someone you can trust. Then, once you decide that you made a good decision, stick with it. Both brokers and lenders are 100% commissioned-based jobs and, like any job, no one likes to work for free. If someone tells me he applied with me and with someone else, I gracefully bow out. In general I'm not interested in working hard for someone if he is not interested in committing to me. It may sound harsh, but step in our shoes. We need to open escrow, title, order the appraisal, meet the clients, collect the appropriate documentation, meet contract contingency dates, write and provide approval letters, get final loan documents out for signing and close on time. I can't afford to spend my time and my company's resources for a "maybe."

Tax Advantages

Obviously, you need a roof over your head.

You get a place to call your own. And when you improve your home, you improve its value. You gain pride of ownership and are part of the American Dream. You're the envy of your friends and family. With a little bit of down payment, you can make a lot of money.

As your property appreciates, you gain a hedge against inflation, i.e., a stepping-stone for your next home purchase. You can't get that by renting.

And then there are the wonderful tax advantages. In reward for owning a home, you get to write-off all of your annual mortgage interest from your gross income.

You can also write-off your state property taxes. Best of all, you can get this benefit on a monthly basis. Let's start here.

If you work for a company, then one of the first things you did was to fill out and sign a W-4 form. This is a government form that indicates how many dependents you have. The more dependents you claim, then the less federal tax you pay. Obviously, if it's just you or you and a spouse, you claim 0, 1 or 2 and you pay more in taxes. Once you own a home, however, you can legally claim up to 9 dependents (talk to your accountant). As a result, you will pay less in monthly taxes and feel a significant increase in your pay. Based on your loan size, your accountant should be able to advise you as to how many dependents you should claim.

Let's do the numbers. Suppose:

Your income = $100,000

Your Accountant can tell you what federal tax bracket you are in. In our example, let's use 33%.

As a result, your Federal Tax per year = $33,000.

Now you buy a house. Sales price = $333,400.

The State Property taxes = (approximately) 1.25% or $4,167 per year (this is tax write-off #1).

The mortgage you get is for $300,000 (assuming 10% down). At 6.5% for a 30-year fixed, the monthly payment = $1,896/month of which $1,616 is interest which = $19,401 per year. (This is tax write-off #2).

Write-off #1 ($4,167) plus write-off #2 ($19,401) = $23,568. This is how much the government lets you reduce your gross income by.

Gross Income =	$100,000
Write-off =	-$23,568
Net Gross Income =	$76,432
X	33% tax bracket
New Federal Tax Liablity =	$25,222

As a result of owning a home and our tax laws, your revised tax liability = $25,222. Compare that to the $33,000 you owed prior to owning.

You save $7,777 per year in taxes or you can say you just gave yourself a raise of $648 per month (7,777/12).

A quicker way to get to this number is to take the amount of the gross write-off ($23,568) and multiply it by your tax bracket (33%), which equals $7,777 per year (same number).

Another way to think of it is that if your mortgage payment is $1,896 per month, effectively, it's really only $1,247/month due to the tax benefit. That's probably close to how much you currently pay in rent.

The pride of home ownership, a roof over your head, a stepping stone, a hedge against inflation, little down payment, tax savings - it's a wonder that everyone doesn't send his landlord a pink slip.

THE INTERNET

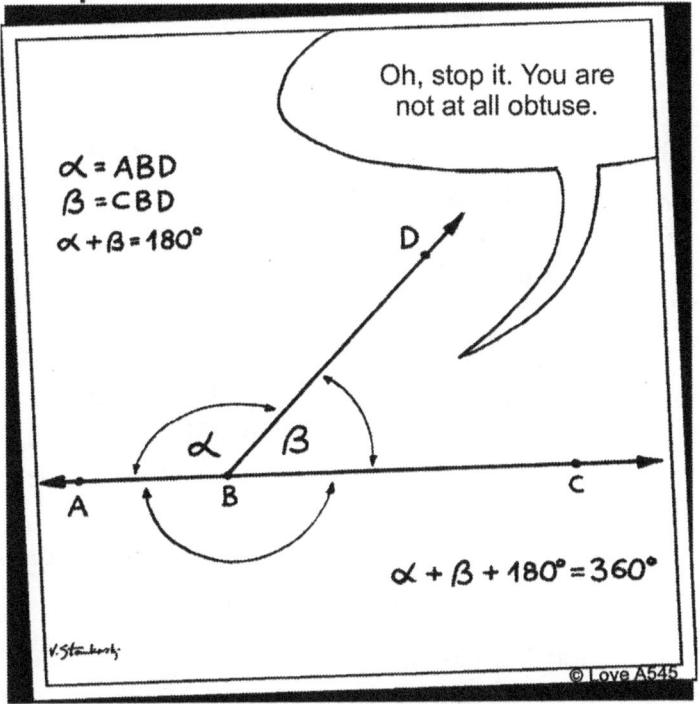

Complimentary angles make the other
angles feel good about themselves.

I'll be brief. As an advertising vehicle for lenders and brokers to seek your business, it's terrific. As a place to find a financial calculator so that you can calculate mortgage payments on a given loan amount or calculate how much you qualify for (conservatively), it's wonderful. As a place to start for comparing rates, 2 thumbs up. As a place to get a loan, it's not good!

Every lender I know has a website that offers you free financial information, a mortgage calculator and today's rates.

www.bankrate.com is a great place to find a mortgage calculator and a place to compare different interest rates per loan product, say all lenders that have a 30-year fixed rate mortgage. If you decide to log on to them, I suggest comparing the rates of the major lenders. They are more scrutinized by the government and are less likely to be tricky. Remember our discussion in the section regarding APR? Different companies use different fees in their calculations and this is often done to get the most attractive rates posted and to get their phone ringing. Remember, a low APR may just mean higher points (fees). Nonetheless, as a comparison tool, it's a good place to start.

Washington Mutual (www.wamumortgage.com) does a nice job of comparing your particular situation with 3 different loan products on a spreadsheet. I'm certain your lender does too.

This is all fine, but when it comes to *applying* for a mortgage, applying for the biggest decision of your life (second biggest), you need to talk to an experienced professional. The majority of my clients have a unique situation that cannot be adequately addressed by the computer. Previously discussed situations (in this book) as part-time jobs, alimony, recently self-employed, history of overtime, gift funds, co-signers, down payment and income averaging are all things that the computer cannot accurately weigh. Hence, when you are all done playing with the computer, pick up the phone and find an experienced mortgage professional.

One more thing you may find interesting. At one of my previous companies, when the market heated up, they received 500 computer-generated mortgage applications per day from applicants requesting to be pre-approved. How much attention do you think these files got once received. I was informed that better than half of these potential clients never received a call back.

In summation, the internet is a great place to learn, just not a great place to apply.

APPRAISAL

Snapshots at jasonlove.com

There is really one primary function that a real estate property appraisal is used for…and it's not to determine whether you got a really good deal. It's to make sure that the lender is not deceived by the unscrupulous. What would life be like without an appraisal? The entire system would collapse from flim-flam buyers and sellers selling real estate at inflated prices only to split the gross profits and allow banks, and the public to take the fall.

99.9% of the time when an honest buyer and seller agree on a value, the appraisal makes (comes in on) the sales price. That's because the buyer and seller, along with the agent, are the market. "Market" here is defined as recently sold homes with similar amenities, in a similar area, selling for similar prices. The key terms are:

1) Similar amenities: homes with approximately the same square footage, lot size, number of bedrooms, baths, pool, fireplace, hardwood flooring, tile roof, garage spaces, a view lot, etc.

2) Similar area: Is the home located south of the boulevard, south of the lake, next to a high school, on a busy street, under a flight path, close to a freeway?

3) Recently sold: Appraisers look at homes that sold in the last 6 months. Older than that and they may not be indicative of current values.

Appraisers assign values to each of these amenities and the value placed on an amenity can change greatly based on location. For instance, a pool in Beverly Hills may be worth an adjustment to value by an increase of $50,000 to $100,000; but in a lower income area, pools are often seen as an unnecessary expense and a dangerous liability. Hence, a buyer in this neighborhood may not recognize value for the pool and neither would the appraiser.

How does an appraiser determine if a particular amenity has value? It's called **Paired Sales Analysis**. In other words, the appraiser does the best job he can to find two sales that are similar and pairs them together. If one property sold for $15,000 more and the only difference between these properties is a pool, then the appraiser would conclude that the pool, in this area, is worth $15,000. Pairing sales can be done for each amenity to determine if the property you are buying is worth more or less than the recent sales in the area based on the attributes of the home you are buying. The following list, contains items that generally add value to a home purchase:

larger lots, larger homes, more bedrooms, superior condition, a pool, a garage vs. carport, a corner lot, a guest house or cabana, architectural appeal, a view

Here's a list of items that would detract from the value of a prospective purchase as compared to other sales in a neighborhood:

smaller in size, inferior condition, 2 bedrooms not 3, property located next to a high school, on a busy street, next to an apartment building, has only a carport vs. garage, has a poor floor plan, smaller lot.

In many ways, anyone can be an appraiser. Just ask yourself if a particular feature makes the property you are looking at more valuable or less.

Here's how it's done. Let's say the house you are buying has a sales price of $300,000.

Amenities:

Pool – yes
Square feet – 1,500
Bedrooms – 3
Baths – 2
Condition – very good

A recent sale in the area (also known as a comparable) sold for $275,000 and had the following amenities:

Pool - no
Square Feet.- 1,400
Bedrooms – 3
Baths – 2.5
Condition – average

The idea is to make the comp (comparable) look exactly like the property we are buying. Add dollars to the comp where there is a noticeable deficiency and subtract where the comp has amenities that are superior. This is done on a spreadsheet typically with 2 more comps. In our example, the adjustments to the comp may look like this.

Add a Pool: + $15,000
100 square feet smaller: (100 square feet at $50/square foot): +$5000
Comp has 1 more bath than subject: -$3,000
Subject property is superior in condition: +$15,000

The net adjustments in this example = +$32,000. Based on the comp, we would say that the subject property, the one we are considering buying, is worth ($275K + $32K) $307,000. If the other two comps adjust out to $295,000 and $302,000, the appraiser would conclude that the sales price is supported and would appraise this property for the sales price ($300,000).

Other than Paired Sales Analysis, there are really two other appraisal theories worth mentioning:

1) Highest and Best Use – if this home is torn down, what should be rebuilt? If it's surrounded by apartment buildings then the answer would be an apartment building, not another house. If it's on a major street, then maybe a parking lot should be built. If the answer is not "house" then the bank is not going to extend financing.

2) Theory of Substitution – states that a reasonable buyer will not pay more for a home than similarly listed homes of equal

size, quality and amenities in the immediate area. Obviously, if a nicer, newly listed home for the same price becomes available, a buyer would substitute this home for the one he is buying.

As an appraiser for over 5 years, there were only two times that I missed a sales price on two separate occasions. The first involved fraud and the Theory of Substitution.

Mr. Badman was buying a home for $425,000 in Sherman Oaks, CA. It was a 1200 square-foot house in average condition. It had a shake roof and a 2 car garage. It sounded a little high at the time, but I didn't think anything about it. While doing my research, however, I discovered a house 1 block away that was 1500 square feet in similar condition with a pool. The "asking" price for this house was only $400,000. At that time, homes were selling for about 5% less than the asking price and a pool was worth a minimum of $10,000. As an appraiser, my job is not to scream "Fraud." It is to determine the value of the property. I appraised it for $400,000 less 5% less $10,000 or $370,000. Needless to say, if the deal closed, it wasn't with my bank.

The second example involves the Theory of Substitution but really is a good example of what happens to out-of -town buyers. Jim and Sue Jacobs were moving from Ohio to Los Angeles. Jim was a successful insurance agent and had a significant income. They were buying in the hills above Sunset Boulevard, an area adjacent to Beverly Hills but with a Los Angeles address. This is a very interesting situation and one that even an experienced buyer might miss. As out-of-towners, the Jacobs don't stand a chance.

There are two types of homes in this neighborhood, homes that are accessible from Beverly Hills and Sunset Boulevard and homes that are accessible from the canyon road to the east which runs north to south connecting the San Fernando Valley to West Los Angeles. The streets above Sunset have names like Thrasher, Blue Jay, and Robbin. They're known as the bird streets. The canyon road is known as Laurel Canyon. This is hard to imagine since these neighborhoods are almost intertwined but simply put, the homes on the bird streets that have direct access to Sunset Boulevard sell for $50,000 to $100,000 more than the homes connected by Laurel Canyon. No matter how hard I tried, I could not find comps. When I called the listing agent asking for help, since we always want to try to make the deal, the agent kept sending me bird street comps. As such, I couldn't use them and appraised the property for $50,000 less than the agreed upon price. This is affectionately known as "killing the deal."

The Jacobs never called me to discuss why I didn't make the sales price. I do not know if they walked from the deal or if they applied for a home loan with someone else. All I know is that out-of-towners really need to come to an area and take some time to drive the area and drive the other recent sales in an area to determine if they are getting a good (reasonable) deal. Relying on the word of a real estate agent with little of your own research is one way to certainly spend more money.

REAL ESTATE AGENTS
(THE GOOD ONES)

Snapshots at jasonlove.com

As I mentioned on the phone, you'll have a spectacular
view of Wildwood Creek ... Of course, next year that
will all just be more tract housing."

OK, so you know how much you can afford and you've decided where you'd like to live. Now it's time to find an agent. There is an old adage that I'm certain everyone has heard by now: 20% of the agents do 80% of the business and 80% of the agents do 20% of the business. Nowhere is that more true then in the real estate industry, including loan officers. Even the L.A. Times once entitled an article "Everyone and Their Grandmother is a Loan Officer." Then the refinance business went away and so did a good 80% of the loan officers. Real estate agents are constantly going away. The average life expectancy of a real estate agent is 3 years. It's a tough job. The commissions are significant...if you make a sale. If not, you're working for free, same as in the mortgage industry. Here are a couple of ideas for finding a successful agent.

1) Ask the loan officer you are working with to see if he can recommend an agent. A good loan officer should be able to refer numerous agents in numerous areas, usually agents that he works with.

2) You can always ask family or friends whom they used. Hopefully, the person they recommend works in the area you'd like to live. If she does not work in that area, then she may be able to refer someone to you who specializes in that location.

3) I suggest driving around the potential areas you'd like to live and counting real estate

agency signs. A large office with a lot of signs may be a good office to give your business to. A large, successful office may have the inside scoop on new listings that are about to hit the MLS (Multiple Listing Service). That's an insider publication that is published for the benefit of the real estate community for all of the agents to see. But a large office that does a lot of listings will announce new listings in their office meeting sometimes more than a week before it gets printed. This may give you an advantage to see and make an offer on a place before the entire real estate industry knows about it. These are sometimes referred to, as pocket listings, since they reside in the hip pocket of the agent until published.

4) Call the chamber of commerce for their ideas and recommendations. They are an excellent source for you to learn about the make-up of a neighborhood including number of people, per-capita income, number of schools, stores and transportation arteries.

5) Check with other like-minded professionals like your accountant, doctor, dentist and insurance agent.

6) If you don't have time to drive through an area, that's OK. There are plenty of

home-buying magazines and, of course, the newspaper. Names of successful agents that do a lot of business will pop out at you as you review potential houses. Give these agents a call. They'll have a pulse on what's going on and what's coming up. There is also a section that congratulates individual agents. I wouldn't necessarily be impressed with this area. It's really used more as an advertising vehicle, and the awards are not always based on merit.

Want a real estate agent to really work hard on your behalf, someone who will spend real time and effort making sure your interest is secured? Once you find a true professional, commit to them as opposed to calling three or four agents. In a 100% commission industry, no one likes to work for free. Commit to one person and that person will be there for you whenever you call her. If she is not, then find a new agent. The good ones live by one simple rule: Do an excellent job and insist on referrals. Excellent means to provide a service that exceeds your expectations. That's how the good ones are able to turn a business into a career. They build a practice based on referrals.

Once you find an agent, be prepared to give her (in writing) your wish list. It's not required, of course, but to have the highest likelihood of finding you the right home, sooner rather than later, you should be able to identify your home in terms of "must have" vs. "negotiable".

Here are some descriptions that may or may not be important to you:

1. 3 bedrooms, not 2
2. has at least 1 1/2 baths
3. Spanish style, but will consider conventional
4. has a pool
5. can be a cosmetic fixer-upper
6. is in a good school district
7. is close to downtown
8. has a 2-car garage
9. has sewer connections vs. septic
10. is on a large lot
11. has a formal dining room
12. has a den or a family room
13. is not more than $450,000 (based on conversation with loan agent)
14. has a view, large lot, curb appeal, etc.
15. is in move-in condition
16. has updated bathrooms/kitchen
17. has hardwood floors and/or tile
18. has master bedroom with master bath
19. is bright and cheery
20. has mature fruit trees
21. has a view or is on a quiet street

The more you can describe it, the quicker you'll find it.

Try to stay away from describing your dream home in terms of square footage. The size of a home is very often determined more by the room count, amenities, and price range. If you are looking for a 3-bedroom house with 2 bathrooms, does it matter if it's 1,500 square feet vs. 1,600 square feet? You probably can't see the difference anyway. Also, be very careful of #19. A new can of paint and some new light-colored carpets can quickly remedy this problem. In fact, most of your wish list can be remedied with money if it pertains to just the house and not to lot size or location. Lot size and location are more like new shoes. They have to fit the first time because they're definitely not getting better.

Before you jump in the car with your agent, make sure you ask her if she has seen it. In a hot market, you may not have a choice. She may have just received notice that this house, the one that meets your list, just came onto the market. Climb in and off you go. Time is of the essence. When I sold my house, the first offer I received was close enough and I accepted it that night. I didn't care if I could have gotten more by waiting. I already bought a new house and wanted to keep things moving forward. The first offer in was the first offer accepted.

In a slow market (see Buyers' and Sellers' Market), let your agent preview the homes for you. It's one of the things they're paid to do. It also insures that you spend your time wisely.

Who Pays the Commission?

When you purchase your dream home, the commission is paid by the seller. It is the standard practice in the state of California and most everywhere else. This presents an interesting dilemma. If the seller is paying the commission, then who are the agents responsible to? Certainly the listing agent is responsible to the seller and yes, technically, your agent is too. Since the seller is the paying client, both agents have the responsibility to try to get the highest possible price for their house. Well then, who's on your side? Many agents will say that a relationship certainly develops between themselves and the buyer. All this is true, and then again, these agents are tired of driving you around. They want their commission. They can taste it! "Just sign here, here, here, here and it's done". Should you pay an extra $10,000? After all, an extra $10,000 is only (approximately) another $68 per month. What do the comps say? Are there like homes in the area that support another $10,000?

Everyone's staring at you. They hand you the pen. What do you do? Bottom line: You're the only one that can say, "I can't afford it. It's not worth it. I won't pay it." And believe it or not, there will be another home that meets your criteria.

My best advice is, keep it analytical. Keep the emotions out of it (as best you can). Don't lose the house because you decided you don't like the seller. Don't lose it because the seller refuses to fix a broken window or a cracked concrete step. Once you have an accepted offer, you can ask for everything to be fixed. If the seller refuses, you probably can fix it cheap. If it's not cosmetic, you can walk. Keep it analytical. Try to avoid these costly comments:

What's another $10,000?
We'll never find the right house.
Our agent's going to hate us.
I'm exhausted. Let's just buy it.

Remember, other than marriage, this is the most difficult and important decision you can make. Take your time and don't feel pressured. At the same time, don't be casual about this process either. Be very methodical about the way you find your new home: preapprove, decide on area, find agent, buy a home.

Buyers' Market vs. Sellers' Market

When meeting an agent you may hear the term, "It's a buyers' market or a sellers' market." When inventory is scarce (not a lot of homes on the market) and you are reading that homes are selling quickly, you can be sure it's a sellers' market. This means prices are higher than normal, homes have multiple offers, and offers are often made higher than the ask price for a home. In this case, you will find it very difficult to control the buying process and your emotions. This experience may be a little disheartening. You may have to review your "list" and make a few more negotiations to get the price down (i.e., 2 bedrooms not 3).

In a buyers' market, the opposite holds true. There are many homes on the market and you can have your choice. Sellers are willing to deal to sell their home quickly. This is a terrific situation for buyers and can be much less frustrating and slower paced. In this market, everyone's your friend. The seller will fix everything. "There's no such thing as too low. Just make an offer. You have to start somewhere...so this market goes.

THE PURCHASE CONTRACT
TIME LINE

"And this must be the pool you mentioned in the ad."

Your agent can provide you with a copy of the purchase contract. Here's a brief overview of the "offer and acceptance" process and what you need to do to be in compliance with your contract (in general). Some dates may vary.

Day 1

All purchase contracts and offers are in writing (by law). Your offer will probably state that the seller has so many hours to accept, reject, or counter your offer. Your offer is accompanied by a 3% earnest money deposit and a pre-approval letter.

Day 2

Your offer is "accepted" or "countered".

Day 3

You accept the counter and escrow is opened. The contract states that escrow is to close in 30, 45, or 60 days (typically). Escrow receives your 3% deposit.

Day 7

If you did not have a pre-approval letter prepared, the contract probably will state that you must have one by now.

Days 7 – 18

Complete all inspections including Home Inspection, Termite Inspection, Soils

Inspection, etc. Accept or reject inspection reports. Request repairs by seller. Waive your financing contingency assuming you have full loan approval including the appraisal report. Return the signed disclosures. Start shopping for Home Owners Insurance. Also Earthquake Insurance if desired. Call a moving company.

If Condominium,

Request Minutes from board meetings and review condo documents (Covenants, Conditions, and Restrictions [CC&R's], budget, and bylaws) as soon as possible. Accept or reject condo documentation. Check for adequate reserves.

Prior to Close of Escrow

Sign your note and deed of trust at escrow. Review estimated settlement statement, which identifies all closing costs. Do walk-through to make sure property is in the same condition as initially seen. Verify that seller repairs have been completed.

At Least 2 Days Before Closing

Wire your funds to escrow or bring a cashier's check. Personal checks not accepted.

Closing Day

Both note and deed of trust records. Pick up your keys. You're MOVING!!

THE HOME INSPECTION

"If we're going to have a banking relationship,
you'll have to trust me more than this."

Home Inspectors are typically recommended by your real estate agent after your offer is accepted. Often, they will mention 2 or 3 companies. You can open the Yellow Pages to find your own inspector or use the one that they recommend. My advice is that you do your research prior to finding your new home.

Please note, these people are not there to tell you if you got a good deal on the house. In fact, they probably won't even know the sales price of the property you just purchased. They won't even care! They are there to tell you the health of your potential new home. What looks good, what needs to be replaced immediately, and how much longer you can expect certain items to last. They may be able to comment on the roof, for instance. But if the roof has issues (ex: water marks on the ceiling), they will probably recommend that you hire a roof inspector. If they see standing water somewhere on the lot, they'll recommend a soil inspection. Usually, they'll spend a lot of time checking that mechanical and electrical hardware are working properly (ex: outlets, range, heater, A/C, pool pumps, filters, plumbing, circuits, circuit breakers and comment whether or not these mechanical systems are up to code.

Take a look at some of the costs that follow. Having a good inspector highlight potential problems can save you a fortune. That's because if a seller wants to sell his house, you can insist that these items be replaced and/or repaired before the close of escrow.

The following data was collected from the Marshall and Swift Contractors book and is based on a 2,000 square foot home with average construction costs:

new roof	$10,000
new plumbing to copper	$4,000
new hot water heater	$500
electrical problems	$80 per hour
replaster pool	$3,500
new heating/cooling system	$4,500
cost to paint	$4,000
new carpeting ($20/yd.)	$3,200
pool equipment	$4,000
new kitchen range	$1,000

All of these items can be negotiated with the seller. If the seller refuses, you are free to cancel escrow and walk away from the deal.

Time to shop for an inspector? Here is a list of questions to ask:

1. How many years in business?
2. What are your professional designations?
3. What items/areas are included/excluded in the inspection?
4. Are you licensed and bonded?
5. When do I receive the report?
6. Will the report identify codes and needed upgrades?
7. Do you provide costs to cure (fix)?
8. Does the report include photographs and or diagrams?

9. How much do you charge?
10. How long does an inspection take?
11. Do you have any literature that you can send me?
12. Is it ok if I walk along with you during the inspection?

I like shopping for an inspector around the same time I'm looking for a home. The fees they charge (buyer pays) will vary and by speaking with two or three of them you can get a good feeling as to their level of competency. Plus, the better outfits will have literature to send you and sometimes a video. Making this up-front effort puts you in charge of the buying process as opposed to relying on others.

How Not to Cancel an Escrow

This is also a good time to discuss how to get out of an escrow and how not to get out of an escrow.

The purchase contract will specifically state how many days you have to perform. By perform, we mean how many days you have to complete all of your inspections which includes having your mortgage loan approved.

Artie and Janice Lassen came to me as a referral from Alex Plat of CB Realtors in Venice, CA. Their offer was accepted at $825,000. And like most first-time buyers, although this was no first-time buyer house, they had second thoughts. "Did we pay too much? Can we afford this after I quit working? Are we buying at the top of the market and are we going to be stuck with a house that is no longer worth what we paid?" The questions didn't stop.

I told them, "Look, if you want out of this escrow, you need to reject the house and cancel this escrow based on your physical inspection report." I should add for those of you reading this that I am not an attorney. There may be other ways to get out of an escrow but the easiest way I know without incurring any costs (penalties) is to reject the physical inspection of the property. "I don't like the report! I want out." It's that easy. Furthermore, if you have 2 weeks to complete your inspections, then you have 2 weeks to get out.

Very often, the financing contingency is 3 weeks. I knew something was up when the Lassens said to me, "If you don't approve us for the loan, then we didn't meet the terms of the contract and we're out, right?"

Most people wanting to buy a home are not this gleeful at the prospect of not being approved.

"Listen," I said. "First of all, we already approved you for the mortgage." I can't arbitrarily unapprove you. If you want out, don't use your financing contingency."

Janice Lassen reminded me that the approval was based on her obtaining a gift from her in-laws and that if the gift was cancelled then the approval was meaningless since the bank requires a minimum of 20% down. She was right about that. We do not do 100% financing on $825,000 homes. And if her gift would have magically disappeared prior to the financing approval date as specified by the contract, she probably would have been fine.

She wasn't fine.

"Richard, my father-in-law can not afford to give us the gift he promised. He was in a terrible accident and will need the money for an operation. Notify the seller that we can't qualify. We are canceling escrow."

I did what she said and let the agents know. However, when it comes to getting your earnest money deposit back out of escrow, that's not so easy. Both the seller and the buyer have to agree to cancel escrow. One party canceling means nothing. The seller sued for failure to perform and wanted compensation. The Lassen's finally got their money back after hiring an attorney and paying $8,000 to the seller plus attorney fees.

THE ESCROW COMPANY

Mr. Adori's Expensive Surprise

It's the end of the road for Mr. Adori and me. It was a 45-day escrow and we are getting ready to close the loan for him and his wife. The excitement was running high as Mr. Adori just learned that their final loan documents arrived in escrow one week before the loan was to fund and close. They always fund first which is the day the lender wires funds to escrow (or the title company) and then legally records, typically the next day, which is the day the deed of trust is entered by the county. In other words, recording means that Mr. Adori is officially the proud new owner.

One week before closing is also the first time Mr. Adori saw a prepared closing statement (a.k.a. estimated Hud 1) by the Excel Escrow Company which reveals not only our bank's fees, which he saw when we first met, but the escrows charges, which he's never saw, reviewed or agreed to. And now he's being asked to sign, pay and close.

"Richard, is this the correct escrow charge, and what is this "Loan Tie In" fee? What is a "Document Preparation" fee? Am I being gouged? The escrow fee is $900.00. The Loan Tie-in fee is $200. There's a Doc Prep fee for $150 and a notary charge for $80. Excluding your fees, they're charging me a whopping $1,330 on a $350,000 sale. Is this correct?"

Wow, that's a lot of eye-opening questions one week before closing. Why wasn't he aware of escrows charges until now? Mr. Adori's closing statement is attached, is correct, and in my opinion is very expensive.

Let's discuss the function of escrow.

The escrow company, by law, is an independent agency that represents the interest of neither the buyer nor the seller. It is completely neutral. It is responsible for following the directions of both parties and will only act in accordance to those directions if both parties (buyer and seller) agree. In other words, you agree to buy the house if both you and the seller agree on:

1) sales price
2) closing date
3) the date by which your financing is to be obtained
4) which inspections are to be performed and by when
5) any other stipulations that are made

In fact, the escrow instructions, those provided by the escrow company, are nothing more than a reprint of your purchase contract. Their responsibility is to insure that both parties meet the terms of the contract. Each party has a fiduciary duty to do so. Either party that fails to perform (per the contract) may be held liable for liquidated damages (monetary compensation).

More importantly, however, is that some escrow companies are more expensive than others. Escrow companies today typically charge between $1.50 to

$2 per thousand based on the sales price, plus another $150 to $200.

Mr. Adori, who is buying his first home found the most expensive one. I shouldn't say he found it. The listing agent selected it and Mr. Adori, exhausted by the home buying process, had no reason to assume he was going to get socked in the end.

The sales price of $350,000 x $2 (per $1,000) = $700 plus an additional $200. Hence, his escrow fee = $900, but it didn't stop there.

Get this: A Loan Tie-in fee is a charge for the service of having you come into the escrow office so that you can sign loan papers. What? At this point you may begin to wonder what was Mr. Adori paying $900 for? I've seen this charge numerous times and I think it's offensive.

Could Mr. Adori have gone to Excel Escrow and pick up his loan documents and have them signed elsewhere one week before closing? You bet! That's exactly what I suggested he do. A traveling notary (yellow pages) will sign you up for $80 to $100 and that includes the notary charge which Excel was charging an additional $80.

The Document Preparation fee is another beauty. Again, it became obvious to Mr Adori that the initial $900 is for nothing. The bank or mortgage company is the one that prepares the loan documents and sends them to escrow. The Escrow Companies now like to charge $150 to $200 to touch the loan papers and figure out how much money you owe? Mind you, I can't claim that Excel is criminal because they are all doing it.

So what should Mr. Adori have done? Shop for an escrow like you shopped for your home but with a lot less leg work. Call several escrow companies in the beginning and let them know you are buying a home in their area. How much will you charge me if I can steer the deal to your office. Will you charge me only $1.50 per thousand and will you waive the Loan Tie-in fee and the Doc-Prep fee? They may not waive it all but you will be pleasantly surprised the savings you can achieve.

What if the seller insists on using their escrow company since selecting this company must be agreed upon? Let the seller know that the company you found has agreed to reduce their fees. That should be ample incentive. If they're still adamant, however, here's one more idea. Call that escrow company. Let them know that you are shopping around and would like to know their costs and if they can be discounted for you. It can't hurt to ask especially if they know that you are considering going with a competitor.

IN CONCLUSION

The Johnsons finally get around
to child-proofing their home.

Getting a mortgage is much like traveling to a foreign country. If you don't read about the customs, the currency exchange and the sites to see, you may just end up in your hotel room calling for room service. How upsetting. You spend a lot of money in airfare just to see what a French Marriott looks like. So to avoid this catastrophe you go to your nearby book store and buy one of the many travel books on the place you are about to visit. Mortgages are no different. To many people, they are foreign. After all, it's not every day that you go out and buy a home. I hope this book serves as your travel guide, from finding the right loan officer, to getting an agent, to closing the deal. Not only is gaining knowledge exciting but as you can see, it can save you a fortune. Now get out there and buy that home!

APPENDIX

The following tables allow you to identify how much loan you qualify for based on a comfortable mortgage payment. Using the following formula accounts for both tax savings (interest write-off) and your monthly obligation for both taxes and insurance. In California, taxes are approximately 1.25% while insurance is roughly .3% per year. This formula is a reprint of that which is found in the Section entitled, "How Much House Can I Afford?"

Here's the formula:

1) Determine a comfortable payment.
2) Add 30% to that payment (by dividing by .70) to compensate for tax savings. Divide by .72 if in a 28% tax bracket, etc. (Talk to your accountant).
3) If you are making a 20% down payment, multiply this new number by .78 to factor out taxes and insurance (which = approximately 22%). Less than 20% down, multiple by .76.
4) This number represents your true comfortable payment after tax savings and takes into account your tax and insurance monthly obligation.
5) Use this number in the following chart to find the mortgage loan that is right for you.
6) Add your down payment to the loan amount to determine your sales price. Divide by .95 for a 5% down payment, by .90 for a 10% down payment, etc.

	5.000	5.125	5.250	5.375	5.500	5.625	5.750	5.875	6.000	6.125	6.250	6.375	6.500	6.625	6.750	6.875	7.000
500	93140	91829	90546	89290	88060	86857	85679	84525	83395	82289	81206	80144	79105	78087	77089	76111	75153
600	111768	110195	108655	107148	105673	104228	102814	101430	100074	98747	97447	96173	94926	93704	92507	91334	90184
700	130397	128561	126764	125006	123285	121600	119950	118335	116754	115205	113688	112202	110747	109321	107925	106556	105215
800	149025	146927	144874	142864	140897	138971	137086	135240	133433	131663	129929	128231	126568	124939	123342	121778	120246
900	167653	165293	162983	160722	158509	156343	154222	152145	150112	148121	146171	144260	142389	140556	138760	137001	135276
1000	186281	183659	181092	178580	176121	173714	171358	169050	166791	164579	162412	160289	158210	156174	154178	152223	150307
1100	204909	202025	199201	196438	193733	191086	188494	185956	183470	181037	178653	176318	174031	171791	169596	167445	165338
1200	223537	220390	217311	214296	211346	208457	205629	202861	200149	197494	194894	192347	189852	187408	185014	182668	180369
1300	242166	238756	235420	232154	228958	225829	222765	219766	216829	213952	211135	208376	205674	203026	200432	197890	195399
1400	260794	257122	253529	250012	246570	243200	239901	236671	233508	230410	227377	224405	221495	218643	215850	213112	210430
1500	279422	275488	271638	267870	264182	260572	257037	253576	250187	246868	243618	240434	237316	234261	231268	228335	225461
1600	298050	293854	289748	285728	281794	277943	274173	270481	266866	263326	259859	256463	253137	249878	246685	243557	240492
1700	316678	312220	307857	303587	299406	295315	291308	287386	283545	279784	276100	272492	268958	265496	262103	258779	255522
1800	335306	330586	325966	321445	317019	312686	308444	304291	300224	296242	292342	288521	284779	281113	277521	274002	270553
1900	353935	348952	344075	339303	334631	330057	325580	321196	316904	312700	308583	304550	300600	296730	292939	289224	285584
2000	372563	367318	362185	357161	352243	347429	342716	338101	333583	329158	324824	320579	316421	312348	308357	304446	300615
2100	391191	385684	380294	375019	369855	364800	359852	355006	350262	345616	341065	336608	332242	327965	323775	319669	315645
2200	409819	404050	398403	392877	387467	382172	376988	371912	366941	362074	357306	352637	348063	343583	339193	334891	330676
2300	428447	422415	416512	410735	405080	399543	394123	388817	383620	378531	373548	368666	363884	359200	354610	350114	345707
2400	447075	440781	434622	428593	422692	416915	411259	405722	400299	394989	389789	384695	379705	374817	370028	365336	360738

The top row represents a range of interest rates while the first column represents your comfortable monthly payment. The intersection of these two rows is your comfortable loan amount.

	5.000	5.125	5.250	5.375	5.500	5.625	5.750	5.875	6.000	6.125	6.250	6.375	6.500	6.625	6.750	6.875	7.000
2500	465704	459147	452731	446451	440304	434286	428395	422627	416979	411447	406030	400724	395527	390435	385446	380558	375768
2600	484332	477513	470840	464309	457916	451658	445531	439532	433658	427905	422271	416753	411348	406052	400864	395781	390799
2700	502960	495879	488949	482167	475528	469029	462667	456437	450337	444363	438513	432782	427169	421670	416282	411003	405830
2800	521588	514245	507059	500025	493140	486401	479802	473342	467016	460821	454754	448811	442990	437287	431700	426225	420861
2900	540216	532611	525168	517883	510753	503772	496938	490247	483695	477279	470995	464840	458811	452904	447118	441448	435891
3000	558844	550977	543277	535741	528365	521144	514074	507152	500374	493737	487236	480869	474632	468522	462536	456670	450922
3100	577473	569343	561387	553599	545977	538515	531210	524057	517054	510195	503477	496898	490453	484139	477953	471892	465953
3200	596101	587709	579496	571457	563589	555887	548346	540962	533733	526653	519719	512927	506274	499757	493371	487115	480984
3300	614729	606075	597605	589315	581201	573258	565482	557868	550412	543111	535960	528956	522095	515374	508789	502337	496014
3400	633357	624441	615714	607174	598813	590630	582617	574773	567091	559568	552201	544985	537916	530992	524207	517559	511045
3500	651985	642806	633824	625032	616426	608001	599753	591678	583770	576026	568442	561014	553737	546609	539625	532782	526076
3600	670613	661172	651933	642890	634038	625373	616889	608583	600449	592484	584684	577043	569558	562226	555043	548004	541107
3700	689241	679538	670042	660748	651650	642744	634025	625488	617128	608942	600925	593072	585380	577844	570461	563226	556138
3800	707870	697904	688151	678606	669262	660115	651161	642393	633808	625400	617166	609101	601201	593461	585878	578449	571168
3900	726498	716270	706261	696464	686874	677487	668297	659298	650487	641858	633407	625130	617022	609079	601296	593671	586199
4000	745126	734636	724370	714322	704487	694858	685432	676203	667166	658316	649648	641159	632843	624696	616714	608893	601230
4100	763754	753002	742479	732180	722099	712230	702568	693108	683845	674774	665890	657188	648664	640313	632132	624116	616261
4200	782382	771368	760588	750038	739711	729601	719704	710013	700524	691232	682131	673217	664485	655931	647550	639338	631291
4300	801010	789734	778698	767896	757323	746973	736840	726918	717203	707690	698372	689246	680306	671548	662968	654561	646322
4400	819639	808100	796807	785754	774935	764344	753976	743824	733883	724148	714613	705275	696127	687166	678386	669783	661353
4500	838267	826466	814916	803612	792547	781716	771111	760729	750562	740605	730855	721304	711948	702783	693804	685005	676384
4600	856895	844831	833025	821470	810160	799087	788247	777634	767241	757063	747096	737333	727769	718400	709221	700228	691414
4700	875523	863197	851135	83932	827772	816459	805383	794539	783920	773521	763337	753362	743590	734018	724639	715450	706445

	7.0	7.125	7.250	7.375	7.500	7.625	7.750	7.875	8.000	8.125	8.250	8.375	8.500	8.625	8.750	8.875	9.000
500	75153	74214	73294	72392	71508	70642	69792	68958	68141	67340	66554	65783	65026	64284	63556	62842	62140
600	90184	89057	87953	86871	85810	84770	83750	82750	81770	80808	79865	78939	78032	77141	76267	75410	74569
700	105215	103900	102612	101350	100112	98898	97709	96542	95398	94276	93175	92096	91037	89998	88979	87978	86997
800	120246	118743	117271	115828	114414	113027	111667	110334	109026	107744	106486	105253	104042	102855	101690	100547	99425
900	135276	133586	131930	130307	128715	127155	125625	124126	122655	121212	119797	118409	117048	115712	114401	113115	111853
1000	150307	148429	146589	144785	143017	141284	139584	137917	136283	134680	133108	131566	130053	128569	127113	125684	124281
1100	165338	163272	161248	159264	157319	155412	153542	151709	149911	148148	146419	144723	143059	141426	139824	138252	136710
1200	180369	178115	175907	173743	171621	169540	167501	165501	163540	161616	159730	157879	156064	154283	152535	150821	149138
1300	195399	192958	190566	188221	185922	183669	181459	179293	177168	175084	173041	171036	169069	167140	165247	163389	161566
1400	210430	207801	205225	202700	200224	197797	195418	193084	190796	188552	186351	184193	182075	179997	177958	175957	173994
1500	225461	222644	219884	217178	214526	211926	209376	206876	204425	202020	199662	197349	195080	192854	190669	188526	186422
1600	240492	237487	234543	231657	228828	226054	223335	220668	218053	215489	212973	210506	208085	205711	203381	201094	198850
1700	255522	252330	249202	246135	243129	240182	237293	234460	231681	228957	226284	223662	221091	218568	216092	213663	211279
1800	270553	267173	263861	260614	257431	254311	251251	248252	245310	242425	239595	236819	234096	231425	228803	226231	223707
1900	285584	282016	278520	275093	271733	268439	265210	262043	258938	255893	252906	249976	247101	244281	241515	238799	236135
2000	300615	296859	293179	289571	286035	282568	279168	275835	272566	269361	266217	263132	260107	257138	254226	251368	248563
2100	315645	311702	307838	304050	300337	296696	293127	289627	286195	282829	279527	276289	273112	269995	266937	263936	260991
2200	330676	326545	322497	318528	314638	310825	307085	303419	299823	296297	292838	289446	286118	282852	279649	276505	273420
2300	345707	341388	337156	333007	328940	324953	321044	317211	313452	309765	306149	302602	299123	295709	292360	289073	285848
2400	360738	356231	351815	347486	343242	339081	335002	331002	327080	323233	319460	315759	312128	308566	305071	301642	298276
2500	375768	371074	366474	361964	357544	353210	348961	344794	340708	336701	332771	328916	325134	321423	317782	314210	310704

	7.0	7.125	7.250	7.375	7.500	7.625	7.750	7.875	8.000	8.125	8.250	8.375	8.500	8.625	8.750	8.875	9.000
2600	390799	385917	381133	376443	371845	367338	362919	358586	354337	350169	346082	342072	338139	334280	330494	326778	323132
2700	405830	400760	395792	390921	386147	381467	376877	372378	367965	363637	359393	355229	351144	347137	343205	339347	335561
2800	420861	415603	410451	405400	400449	395595	390836	386169	381593	377105	372703	368386	364150	359994	355916	351915	347989
2900	435891	430446	425110	419879	414751	409723	404794	399961	395222	390573	386014	381542	377155	372851	368628	364484	360417
3000	450922	445289	439769	434357	429052	423852	418753	413753	408850	404041	399325	394699	390160	385708	381339	377052	372845
3100	465953	460132	454427	448836	443354	437980	432711	427545	422478	417510	412636	407855	403166	398565	394050	389621	385273
3200	480984	474975	469086	463314	457656	452109	446670	441337	436107	430978	425947	421012	416171	411422	406762	402189	397701
3300	496014	489818	483745	477793	471958	466237	460628	455128	449735	444446	439258	434169	429177	424279	419473	414757	410130
3400	511045	504661	498404	492271	486259	480365	474587	468920	463363	457914	452569	447325	442182	437136	432184	427326	422558
3500	526076	519504	513063	506750	500561	494494	488545	482712	476992	471382	465879	460482	455187	449993	444896	439894	434986
3600	541107	534347	527722	521229	514863	508622	502503	496504	490620	484850	479190	473639	468193	462850	457607	452463	447414
3700	556138	549190	542381	535707	529165	522751	516462	510295	504248	498318	492501	486795	481198	475706	470318	465031	459842
3800	571168	564033	557040	550186	543466	536879	530420	524087	517877	511786	505812	499952	494203	488563	483030	477599	472271
3900	586199	578876	571699	564664	557768	551007	544379	537879	531505	525254	519123	513109	507209	501420	495741	490168	484699
4000	601230	593719	586358	579143	572070	565136	558337	551671	545133	538722	532434	526265	520214	514277	508452	502736	497127
4100	616261	608562	601017	593622	586372	579264	572296	565463	558762	552190	545745	539422	533219	527134	521164	515305	509555
4200	631291	623405	615676	608100	600674	593393	586254	579254	572390	565658	559055	552579	546225	539991	533875	527873	521983
4300	646322	638248	630335	622579	614975	607521	600213	593046	586019	579126	572366	565735	559230	552848	546586	540442	534412
4400	661353	653091	644994	637057	629277	621650	614171	606838	599647	592594	585677	578892	572236	565705	559298	553010	546840
4500	676384	667934	659653	651536	643579	635778	628129	620630	613275	606062	598988	592048	585241	578562	572009	565578	559268
4600	691414	682777	674312	666004	657881	649906	642088	634422	626904	619530	612299	605205	598246	591419	584720	578147	571696
4700	706445	697620	688971	680493	672182	664035	656046	648213	640532	632999	625610	618362	611252	604276	597432	590715	584124
4800	721476	712463	703630	694972	686484	678163	670005	662005	654160	646467	638920	631518	624257	617133	610143	603284	596552
4900	736507	727306	718289	709450	700786	692292	683963	675797	667789	659935	652231	644675	637262	629990	622854	615852	608981
5000	751537	742149	732948	723929	715088	706420	697922	689589	681417	673403	665542	657832	650268	642847	635565	628421	621409

Mr. Adori's Settlement Statement

Contract Sales Price $350,000

Down Payment $35,000

Bank Charges
Loan origination (1 pt) $3,150
Underwriting Fee $430
Appraisal fee $325
Tax procurement $81
Flood Certificate $13
Credit Report $8
Wire Fee $35

New Loan Charges (Subtotal) $4,042

Prepaid Interest from
10/15 – 11/1 $721

Hazard Insurance (fire) $870

Settlement Charges
Escrow fee $900
Doc Prep fee $150
Loan Tie In $200
Notary $80
Fed Express $25
Copying/fax $30

Settlement Charges (Sub Total) $1,385

Title Insurance and Recording
Lenders Coverage $462
Endorsements $75

County Recording fee $68

Title Charges (Sub Total) $605

Closing Costs (Subtotal) $7,623

FUNDS REQUIRED TO CLOSE $42,623

ABOUT THE AUTHOR

I started in the Real Estate business in 1987. Back then I was hired by Home Fed. Bank and was trained as an appraiser. In 1990, I switched companies and appraised for Citibank. In mid-1991, I attended a Citibank meeting with the mortgage loan officers at an offsite hotel. They had breakfast, omelets, fresh fruit, rolls and warm muffins. They laughed and appeared to be having much fun, a lot more fun than any meeting I had attended with the appraisers. That was it. In 1991, after already passing several appraisal competency exams, I decided to jump to the loan origination department and start over as a home loan officer for Citibank. I worked there until 1993, when I was offered a position with PNCMortgage, one of the biggest regional banks in the country. In 1997, I was made an Area Sales Manager and still maintained my production. In 1998 and 1999, I was the top loan officer for PNC in Southern California. In February 2001, the mortgage division of PNC was purchased by Washington Mutual, where I maintained my production and continued making President's Club, an honor awarded to less than 5% of the company nationwide. In that time, I can truly say that I've learned a few things that I'm happy to share.

www.ingramcontent.com/pod-product-compliance
Lightning Source LLC
Chambersburg PA
CBHW021954170526
45157CB00003B/988